A Nation of Strangers was first published by the Museum of Photographic Arts on the occasion of the three-part exhibition series POINTS OF ENTRY, created by the Museum of Photographic Arts, San Diego; the Center for Creative Photography. Tucson; and The Friends of Photography, San Francisco.

Michael Read, POINTS OF ENTRY
    Publication Coordinator
Rupert Jenkins, POINTS OF ENTRY
    Production Editor
Designed by Toki Design, San Francisco

© 1995 by Museum of Photographic Arts

Library of Congress Catalog Card Number
95-076802

Printed in Hong Kong by C & C Printing Co., Ltd.

Reprinted 1997 by the University of
New Mexico Press

Second printing, 1998

ISBN 0-8263-1833-9

A NATION OF STRANGERS

Essays by Vicki Goldberg and Arthur Ollman

Bibliography by Catherine S. Herlihy

Museum of Photographic Arts   *San Diego*

University of New Mexico Press   *Albuquerque*

POINTS OF ENTRY has been made possible by a major grant from the Lila Wallace—Reader's Digest Fund

The entire POINTS OF ENTRY three-part exhibition series, catalogues, national tour, and educational programming has been made possible by a major grant from the

LILA WALLACE — READER'S DIGEST FUND

A Nation of Strangers
Reframing America
Tracing Cultures

Additional support for the national tour and promotion of POINTS OF ENTRY has been generously provided by ❊ **Metropolitan Life Foundation**

The publication and distribution of the curriculum resource for teachers in San Diego and surrounding communities was made possible by the Weingart Foundation and the Elizabeth Firestone Graham Foundation.

POINTS OF ENTRY National Tour

Museum of Photographic Arts
San Diego, California
September, 1995

International Museum of Photography
   at George Eastman House
Rochester, New York
April, 1996

The Jewish Museum
New York, New York
May, 1997

Center for Creative Photography
Tucson, Arizona
September, 1995

National African American
   Museum Project
Smithsonian Institution
Washington, DC
August, 1996

Center for the Fine Arts
Miami, Florida
September, 1997

The Friends of Photography/
   Ansel Adams Center for Photography
San Francisco, California
September, 1995

High Museum of Art\
   Nexus Contemporary Art Center
Jimmy Carter Presidential
   Library-Museum
Atlanta, Georgia
February, 1997

A NATION OF STRANGERS Solo Tour

The Museum of Tolerance
Simon Wiesenthal Center
Los Angeles, California
March, 1998

Ellis Island Immigration Museum
New York, New York
May, 1998

THIS CATALOGUE DOCUMENTS ONE OF THREE EXHIBITIONS that together constitute POINTS OF ENTRY, a unique collaboration among three photography museums intended to focus attention on one of the central defining issues of American life: immigration.

Photography can teach us a great deal about what immigration means within the context of American culture. For the past century and a half, photographers have documented the faces and experiences of those who immigrated to this country. Many of America's finest photographers have been immigrants themselves, and the work they produced in this country has expanded our artistic boundaries and deepened our understanding of the complexities and contradictions inherent to a nation of immigrants. And today, many younger artists are looking at the experience of immigration as a key to comprehending their own cultural heritages and identities.

As a series, POINTS OF ENTRY seeks to expand the discussion about the meanings and impact of immigration through photography. Some of those photographs are historical images found in archives across the country, some are among the classic works of art of the twentieth century, some have been created by a new generation of artists. Together they constitute a rich panorama of artistic responses to the subject of immigration and cultural differences.

To create such a complex and important project, three museums in three different communities joined together in a collaborative effort, supported by a major grant from the Lila Wallace–Reader's Digest Fund and with additional support from Metropolitan Life Foundation. The Museum of Photographic Arts (San Diego) initiated the collaboration and secured the project funding. The exhibitions, catalogues, and programming were created and produced in a partnership that involved the artistic and administrative staffs of the Museum of Photographic Arts, the Center for Creative Photography (Tucson), and The Friends of Photography (San Francisco).

We are profoundly grateful to the Lila Wallace–Reader's Digest Fund for its visionary grant, which enabled the consortium to take the risk to create POINTS OF ENTRY, and to Metropolitan Life Foundation, which stepped forward to support the national tour and its promotion at a crucial time in its development. Among the exceptional collaborators on the project have been Vicki Goldberg, guest curator for the Museum of Photographic Arts; Andrei Codrescu, Rebecca Solnit, and Ronald Takaki, guest essayists for the catalogues; and Catherine S. Herlihy, bibliographer. We thank them for their contributions, as we thank the literally hundreds of others across the country who provided support, guidance, advice, contacts, original art, and loans of historical materials.

The American public today is being exposed to a wide range of information and opinions about immigration and its impact on our culture. Many of the debates now taking place have roots that extend deep into American history. We hope that the efforts of the artists, scholars, writers, and researchers presented here will promote a fuller understanding of the richness of the American cultural experience, past, present, and future.

Arthur Ollman, Director, Museum of Photographic Arts
Andy Grundberg, Director, The Friends of Photography
Terence Pitts, Director, Center for Creative Photography

CONTENTS

This is the story of everyone, the tale of all of us together. The personal, private story of all Americans living and dead. How we came to be here. How we became who we are. This is the story that each one of us owns, told and retold—wrapped in hardship, in pain, in tears, in triumphs over impossible odds. Here are the groups, conquered and unconquered, the empowered, and the powerless. This is the saga of a disparate nation. No individual may tell of it so that it can be recognized by the rest of us. We each hold a piece of the mosaic, and none can see the whole image. This is the story of every one of us, a nation of strangers.

This is the land of boundless rhetoric. Here, hopes and expectations reach new and surreal levels. America the virginal land, accessed by Golden Gates, leading to mountains of gold, flowing with milk and honey. A haven of perfect freedom, an harmonious convergence of all the earth's peoples, where the last and the least have become the first and the most. Free land and absolute opportunity, limited only by one's own vision and will, where a new people, reflecting the finest qualities of the earth's most motivated and self selected, succeed in any endeavor. Here the lions lay with the lambs. Here, no tempest tossing. All gods, at peace with one another.

Astoundingly, there have been some for whom this hyperbole came true, at least in large part. Such rhetoric could only expect to fail for nearly everyone else. Most came to find a better life. Others were forcibly brought here to provide it. This land extracted their life blood and paid out bitterness.

The first dwellers in America were Asiatic tribes crossing the Bering Strait, but native peoples have many other arrival legends: some recall arrival from the East with the sun, others sprouted from roots among the corn, some from rain. For hundreds of generations, these tribes migrated and populated this hemisphere.

The early history of the United States represents the efforts of principally western European immigrants to establish a home, based on freedoms and opportunities they were unable to obtain in Britain, France, Holland, Germany, and Spain. Some were sent officially on missions of conquest, others were fleeing domination in their homelands. There was little consistency in their vision of the future.

Visual evidence of the earliest periods of immigration is scarce. Photography arrived in the U.S. immediately

BY ARTHUR OLLMAN

Facing page: **G. R. Hall**, after Alonzo Chappel, *Landing of Roger Williams*, 1857. Checklist #14

By any standard we are all immigrants. Even the tribes of native peoples, who have resided here for millennia, have arrival legends. While many trace their tribal memories to the West, others in New England describe ancestors arriving from the East across the Atlantic. Europeans heroicized and mythologized their arrival, although few now maintain the preposterous version depicted here.

after its announcements in France and England in the year 1839. By that date, some European families had been on this continent for more than two hundred years. The U.S. population was principally white, western and northern European, and Protestant. The vast majority of early American photographs depict people who are several generations past immigration. Nevertheless, from the mid-nineteenth century to the present, photographers have found the new arrivals irresistible subjects. The ways in which we interpret photographs of immigrants are closely tied to our own perception of the immigrant experience. The images, in all their diversity, identify both the American Dream and its corollary nightmare.

From pre-colonial times to the present, there has been free and unfree movement of people; there are those who chose to be here and others whose identity as Americans was forced upon them.

Between 1619, when the first Africans were brought here, and 1865, more than ten million Africans were sold to the Americas, leaving at least one million dead in the deep Atlantic. Over six hundred thousand arrived on soil that later became the United States. Torn from their homes, they were not only exiled from their tribes, their loved ones (both living and ancestral), their cultures, and their languages, they had also lost their topography, seasonal cycles, weather patterns, foods, and fauna. Significantly, even the stars of the heavens that guided them physically and spiritually—that they prayed to, knew

their seasons by, named, and mythologized—even those were gone in their new northern hemisphere sky. If they could survive their capture and the deadly slave ships, the long anticipated arrival only produced for them a world of misery, terror, and a separation from the open practice of their religion. As religious people the world over confirm, the only thing worse than a life of pain and abuse is the degradation of one's spiritual life. Africans arrived facing as many as fifteen generations of forced slavery and systematic punishment. Having no control over their fate, their identity, their labor, or even their children, Africans provide the most egregious and notorious example of forcible immigration in U.S. history.

The earliest Africans came along with Europeans to the colonies as indentured servants who obtained their freedom after a proscribed period of labor. In 1660, colonial records show, Africans and Europeans were indentured in equal numbers. Within several years the laws of the colonies were changed to mandate specified periods of service for Europeans, but service in perpetuity—to include any offspring—for Africans. It is estimated that by 1800, one-half to two-thirds of all European Americans had arrived as indentured servants. Free Blacks and their progeny numbered nearly half a million by the Civil War. Three out of four whites in the South never held slaves, but the all-pervasive, pernicious culture of slavery extended to all quarters of society. Immigrant, indentured and slave labor fueled America's burgeoning economy.

All early arrivals came on sailing vessels. The New England trade routes to Northern Europe provided numerous cargo ships, each with a small number of berths for travelers. The voyage was unpredictable, dangerous and costly. The ships were ill-equipped to handle passengers. In such vessels, the Irish began arriving in the late 1820s in New York, Boston, and Philadelphia. So dangerous was the sail crossing of the Atlantic that sixteen percent of the Irish who attempted to come to America died at sea. In fact, some literally died in Boston harbor. Hatred of the Irish was so extreme that every effort was made to block their coming ashore. In the 1830s and 1840s, they experienced anti-Irish riots, arrests, murders, and the burning of Catholic churches. Labeled vermin and maggots in the press, the Irish became a despised lower class. Often, when jobs needed to be done that would put the lives of slaves at risk, Irish were hired to perform them. A common expression in the nineteenth century was "You seldom see a gray-haired Irishman." The average Irish immigrant lived forty years; these most rural Europeans became the most urban Americans.

In Boston, the previous lowest class had been small numbers of free Blacks who had been settled there for years, even since colonial times. Conflicts between African Americans and Irish Americans over the subtle distinction of who would reside at the bottom of the heap were bitter and durable. The residue of this hatred is still played out periodically in that

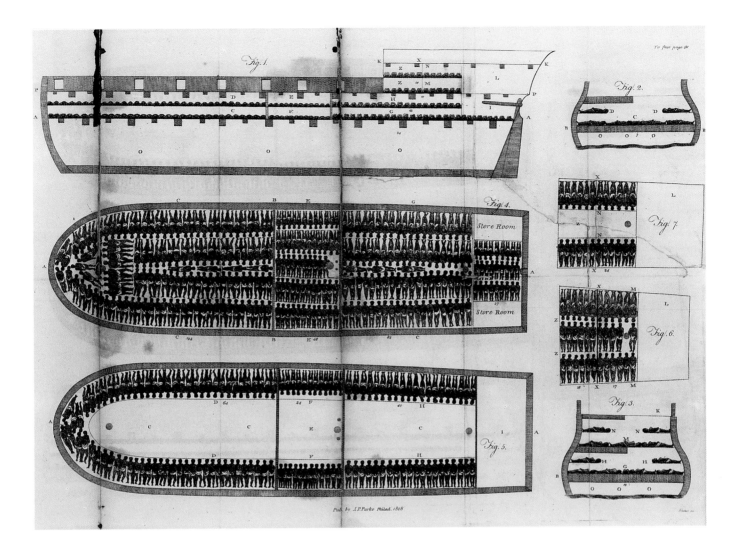

Unknown artist, Untitled (cutaway sectional renderings of slave ship), 1808, printed later. Checklist #2

This infamous image, showing how slaves were stored for the long sea voyage, coldly reveals the horror and inhumanity of this commerce.

city and in New York, where the Draft Riots of 1863 unleashed the worst urban violence in American history, pitting Irish immigrants against African Americans.

In 1849 gold was discovered in California, and word of it traveled to Asia as fast as it did to Europe. Three hundred and twenty-five of the "forty-niners" came from China. By 1870 there were sixty thousand Chinese in America.[1] They made exotic subjects for photography, and today many photographs of them survive.

Thousands of young Chinese men chose to come here, expecting to sojourn in America for a number of years to work, save, and return to a better life in China. In the 1850s in China, teenagers—and often children—were captured on the streets and even in their homes and sold into contract labor in America. These "shanghaied" unfortunates never returned to their families, were sequestered in squalid mining camps and "Chinatowns" and denied every freedom, according to U.S. law. Segregation of Chinese from American opportunity regularly drew them into poverty, disillusionment, and immobility. The vast majority of these people devoted their lives to building the American

Unknown artist, *C. T. Sampson's Shoe Manufactory with Chinese Shoemakers in Working Costume, North Adams, Massachusetts,* c. 1875. Checklist #30

Before the Chinese Exclusion Act of 1882 was implemented (a law which prohibited all Chinese immigration to the U.S.), only male Chinese laborers were allowed to immigrate; their wives and children were not. The imbalance in Chinese male/female population ratios in the U.S. was more extreme than many other immigrant groups. By 1890, Chinese men outnumbered Chinese women in this country by 27 to 1. As a result of this imbalance, there was no sizeable second generation (American-born children of Chinese immigrants) until after the Exclusion Act was finally repealed in 1943.

Source: *Ethnic America: A History,* Thomas Sowell, 1981, Basic Books, Inc., pg. 140–41

infrastructure and died impoverished in Chinese ghettos.

Chinese and Irish workers were manipulated into angry confrontations by industrialists seeking the cheapest labor supply in the 1870s. Low wages, job insecurity in the face of mechanization, and dangerous working conditions—particularly in the shoe-making industry—led to the formation of the Irish Union, the Secret Order of the Knights of St. Crispin. With more than fifty thousand members, it was the largest labor union in the United States. In 1870, the Crispins struck for an eight-hour workday at Sampson's Shoe Factory in North Adams, Massachusetts. Seventy-five Chinese workers were brought in as scabs from San Francisco. By proving their productivity and willingness to work long hours at low wages, they broke the strike. The success of this union-busting strategy was repeated again and again in that industry and others. Management hailed the Chinese as the "final solution" to the labor problem in America.[2] In similar ways, Chinese labor replaced plantation workers after the Civil War. In their turn, Japanese, Koreans, Latin Americans, Caribbeans, and Filipinos replaced Chinese workers in industry and agriculture. Each new group was exploited until it could represent its own concerns in law and legislation. Today, most of these groups still lag far behind national averages in income, wages, and benefits.

The Chinese Exclusion Act of 1882 was the first piece of national legislation governing immigration.

Until then, no one arrived here illegally. The exclusion act made Chinese ineligible for citizenship as well as for entry. Many subsequent laws were passed all over the country restricting the rights of anyone "ineligible for citizenship." The Cable Act of 1922 even stipulated that any American woman marrying an individual who was not eligible for citizenship "shall cease to be a citizen of the United States." It was not until 1943 that the Cable Act was repealed, finally extending naturalization rights to Chinese already here. Allowances were made for a paltry 105 Chinese to immigrate to the U.S. annually. The repeal was a small and overdue reward for a century of loyalty and labor, and was precipitated by China's support of the Allies in WWII.

America has grown and prospered even as it has often abused its very builders. But the resulting nation has been soundly built and it functions well for much of its population, the sons and daughters of immigrants. Its enormous energy and sense of opportunity for newcomers exert a strong gravitational seductivity around the globe. Photographs from the 1840s to the present illustrate earnest immigrants, eager to join the American enterprise. Such photographs were central to all efforts to attract newcomers. One may view these immigrants as crude, dim, and unassimilable—or as proud, potent, and patriotic, according to the politics of the time. The fact remains that our comforts and freedoms were provided by them.

Northern and western European settlers could obtain cheap or even free land in the nineteenth century. A homesteader could bite off all he could chew in many fertile areas and occasionally choke on some desolate stretches. This land, however, had already been occupied by sophisticated societies of indigenous peoples. As wave after engorged wave of diverse newcomers crashed ashore, increasingly barbaric and clever methods were employed to destroy the resident occupants and replace them on the land. Photographs of prosperous settlers in the American prairies were circulated through Scandinavia and Germany, luring many to immigration ports.

United States immigration, until the advent of steam-powered ships, came largely along our trade routes. Steam ships were much larger, more profitable to operate, and could predictably cross the Atlantic in less than one-third of the time required of sailing ships. With cheaper fares people could set out for America at a fraction of earlier costs. Large numbers of southern and eastern Europeans began arriving in the 1880s. Their cultural differences were perceived as extreme, and like previous arrivals they were deemed unassimilable. Their histories, traditions, languages, and religious practices repelled those already on shore. The largest of these groups were Italians and Jews. In 1902, Woodrow Wilson wrote in his *History of the American People:* "The immigrant newcomers of recent years are men of the lowest class from the South of Italy, and men of the meaner sort out of Hungary and Poland, men out of the ranks where there was neither skill nor energy, nor any initiative of quick intelligence."

While many northern Europeans, particularly Scandinavians and Germans, selected farm and ranch land in the mid-western States, the Irish, Italians, Jews, and many other southern and eastern Europeans settled in the eastern port towns where they arrived. Not only had their stamina and their money run out, but predecessors from their own families and villages had already begun to establish themselves in neighborhoods like the Lower East Side of New York.

"I came to America because I had heard the streets were paved with gold, and I found three things. One: The streets were not paved with gold. Two: The streets were not paved at all. Three: I was expected to pave them."—Italian Immigrant, 1903[5]

These new arrivals saw that the streets were filled with opportunity, a product in miserably short supply where they had come from, but in order to access it, they first needed to cross the threshold, at Ellis Island.

Ellis Island was a great testing ground. Poor immigrants were well aware that they would be closely scrutinized by officials there, and that they might well be denied admission and sent back. Their vulnerability provided a concise window on their cultural preferences and ideals. Immigrants hoped to show themselves as healthy, industrious, and morally fit, and they identified their strengths in the only way they knew. Disembarking in their finest and often ceremonial clothing, they demonstrated the profound importance of this moment of presentation and judgement.

Portraits made by Augustus Sherman—for thirty-seven years an employee at Ellis Island—and later Lewis Hine, show the most earnest, hopeful arrivals, arrayed in international splendor. They displayed rich embroidery, lederhosen, animal-skin vests, high hats, starched pleated collars, but often, sadly, many were bedraggled individuals who wore their only torn and stained outfits.

"When I was a little boy I would hear stories of how my family travelled from Grodno, Russia. The older relatives told of how the family had nothing to bring with them, and of leaving Grodno with an empty suitcase they borrowed so no one would know they had no worldly possessions."—Joel Greenberg, grandson of Rose Greenberg, a Russian Jewish immigrant, c. 1915.[4]

The very identifiers that illustrated capability and strength in "the old country" often produced opposite responses here. A fine goatskin vest, a prized possession in the Carpathian Mountains, made one appear a foreign "bumpkin," ripe for fleecing on the Lower East Side of New York or Maxwell Street in Chicago.

People came bearing the attitudes and prejudices of their homelands; a northern Italian arrived in Chicago feeling superior to a southern, darker skinned Italian and therefore also to a darker Dominican, Puerto Rican, or Navajo. Skin color is not the only identifier of discrimination. German

Jews who had settled in New York in the mid-nineteenth century were repulsed by the less educated "crude" Jews of Russia arriving a generation or two later. The English often felt superior to Irish immigrants, regardless of class or accomplishment.

Numerous immigrant groups have never been expected to blend into the general society. They have been systematically excluded from any of its benefits. For them the loss of tradition and cultural identity is particularly painful. For many Americans of color, the history and promise of the United States is thus not identified by the earnest faces awaiting entry at Ellis Island. It may instead be seen in photographs of slaves; or in an image from the 1940s of a highly polished FBI operative rifling through family albums in a Japanese American home, searching for subversive materials as the dispirited family watches helplessly from their dining table; or in the handsome, hopeful face of an undocumented Mexican worker, emerging from a tunnel under the new, ineffectual border fence near San Diego.

People of many traditions never find the respect of their neighbors that they enjoyed abroad. Their social exclusion may be caused by the very qualities they perceive as their finest. Never invited to join the community mosaic, and having lost their natural home, they are true exiles, starved for meaning in a land of plenty. To dishonor their motives for coming here, and to minimize the effort they have expended to benefit all of us, is to distort our national his-

tory and disparage our own immigrant ancestors. Our labors and successes are built largely on their labors and successes.

Labor and immigration are linked throughout our history. While jobs are a magnet for the newcomer, organized labor has always been one of the most vigilant of America's gatekeepers. Relegated to entry level positions, new arrivals generally sell their labor cheaply. Whether the immigrant is uneducated or a Ph.D., he or she will rarely enter the market at the highest level. Current policies are bringing some of the best prepared and best educated immigrants in our history to the U.S., many of whom will initially work at or near the bottom of the wage scale. This positioning threatens labor unions. Traditionally, employers and the government have worked in concert to design an immigrant flow that keeps the cost of goods and services low. Americans have come to rely on these cost structures even as they may resent and resist the immigrants themselves.

Laborers are generally shown in early photographs as heroic, monumental titans conquering mountains of logs, erecting glorious bridges, boiling hogs by the ton, laying thousands of miles of track; proud, strong, capable, humble. Working immigrants were needed to quickly and efficiently fill the vacuum left by the removal of native peoples from their lands, and to supply a growing and hungry nation. Theirs were the first plows to open the plains, but that land had been religiously stewarded by stable hunter/gatherer societies for centuries. The photographs show no sense of previous occupancy, only the present noble resident building his new version of America.

Becoming citizens by having the identity of one's land changed was the common experience of native peoples on this continent, as well as for the French citizens of Louisiana, the people of Puerto Rico, Hawaiian Islanders, Alieuts of Alaska, and many Mexicans of the Southwest. These citizens are not considered immigrants. For generations they had occupied land that became part of the United States as the borders changed around them. In 1848, at the time of the Treaty of Guadalupe-Hidalgo, which ended the war with Mexico, about twenty thousand Mexicans lived in California. Because of the discovery of gold a year later, California was quickly granted statehood, in September of 1850. Another sixty thousand Mexicans lived in New Mexico when the Treaty of Guadalupe-Hidalgo was signed, making New Mexico a U.S. territory. New Mexico was not granted statehood until 1912, though it satisfied all the legal requirements in 1848. The granting of statehood was withheld, as was done later with the state of Hawaii, until the state's population was sufficiently "American." The Mexican American community is, therefore, one of the oldest and one of the newest in America.

In 1924, the first border patrol unit was formed, but the Mexican frontier was largely ignored until World War II. Thousand of workers crossed daily in both directions, unchecked. For

Augustus Sherman, *Gypsy family at Ellis Island*, c. 1910. Checklist #57

Estimates of the number of Gypsies in the U.S. range between 500,000 and one million. Gypsies refer to themselves as "Rom," which is a Hindi word for "man." Their language is derived from a dialect related to Sanskrit. According to the 1970 census, "Rom" was the primary language of only 1,599 people living in America. Originating in India, Gypsies fled persecution in the eighth century and again in the eleventh century. They moved to Persia, Turkey, and Egypt before settling in Europe. The Europeans named them "Gypsies," a bastardization of the word "Egyptians." Their history is marked by persecution. It is estimated that approximately one million Gypsies were killed by the Nazis during WWII.

John Vachon, *Mexican and Negro farm labor, Corpus Christi, Texas*, 1943, printed later. Checklist #122

John Vachon was an important member of the Farm Security Administration photography team, along with Russell Lee, Arthur Rothstein, Carl Mydans, Dorothea Lange, Marion Post Wolcott, Theo Jung, Ben Shahn, Walker Evans, Paul Carter, Arthur Siegel, Jack Delano, and John Collier, Jr., all under the direction of Roy Stryker. A government program, the Farm Security Administration was designed to document conditions of poverty during the Great Depression.

much of this century Mexican laborers have been brought to the U.S. by the trainload, recruited by U.S. farmers. The pathway to *El Norte* was well paved by American industrial and agricultural needs, and by the desires of motivated Mexican workers for a better life. During World War II, to replace American men fighting overseas, over a hundred thousand Mexican families were induced to bring in crops and work in factories all over the United States. In the 1950s many were deported. Substantial numbers of U.S. citizens of Mexican ancestry were also deported. Their services were no longer essential, and public sentiment moved against them.

As the two nations lie side by side, touching, loving, fighting, the United States and Mexico represent different views of the world. Joined by history, need, and trade agreements, we have not learned to trust each other. Mexico sees our Yankee smugness, our

hegemony, our fierce gravitational influence, and a history of armed intervention. We see millions of undocumented workers and a fear of millions more in an inexorable de facto national reclamation of their original cultural boundaries. Each nation is quick to blame the other in times of crises. "It's not a border, it's a scar," writes Carlos Fuentes.[5]

The complexities of this region can no longer tolerate nativist sound-bite solutions and punitive scapegoating legislation, designed solely to elect fearmongers. Any lasting solutions must be arrived at bilaterally.

As the progeny of many nations arrived, each for unique reasons, a new society was formed. The resulting mix was little devoted to the concerns of each narrow component.

"Other nations had large homogeneous native populations. . . . In such societies newcomers were truly foreigners, outsiders who must somehow penetrate thickly interwoven norms, styles, and beliefs before gaining acceptance. But Americans could not delude themselves with a unifying myth; their ethnic, religious and cultural diversity was too plain to be ignored. . . . It was not to protect others, but to protect themselves, and their own right to differ, that Americans were tolerant."— Thomas Kessner, "Immigration and the American Experience."[6]

Jewish immigrant Emma Lazarus' sonnet on the Statue of Liberty announced to the world the radical notion that the tired and poor, the yearning huddled masses, the wretched refuse, the homeless, could here be healed and transformed by the simple application of medicinal liberty. Four years before the Statue of Liberty's unveiling, however, Congress had passed its first major immigration law, halting absolutely the entry of Chinese immigrants. It also excluded convicts, the insane, and those unable to support themselves.

Responding to popular concerns about huge numbers of immigrants, sprawling ghettos, depressed wages, and nativist racism, Congress, in the 1920s, passed a series of federal laws severely restricting immigration. The time of huge immigration ended.

"Diversity had contributed to the evolution of American liberty. Over the years they (immigrants) peopled the land, pushed back its frontiers, built its cities, laid its tracks, worked its factories, enriched its culture, and fashioned a remarkable technology. They had also reaped concomitant benefits: liberty, the ability to aspire for a better life and (for even a poor child) to dream ample but attainable dreams. But as the dreams came true and immigrants became successful Americans, many forgot the awkwardness, the difficulties associated with the process of immigration and assimilation and the making of new cultures and traditions. And now they feared it. So the doors were closed."— Thomas Kessner, "Immigration and the American Experience."[7]

So tightly were the doors closed that even during World War II, when millions of Europeans needed to be sheltered, America allowed in even fewer than the legally prescribed quota. Escaping from Nazi Germany,

a large group of German Jews managed to sail to the U.S. in 1939 aboard the *St. Louis.* Anchoring close enough to Miami Beach to hear music from the resorts, they were not allowed to come ashore as refugees. Ultimately, the ship was forced to return to Europe, where most of the passengers died in Hitler's camps.

Only very select artists, literati, and scientists were allowed to enter. This influx of intellectual capital, in short order, created the atomic bomb, reinvented world architecture, made New York the center of the art world, and established important schools. European photographers such as André Kertész, Lisette Model, Marion Palfi, John Gutmann, László Moholy-Nagy, Man Ray, Alexei Brodovitch, Robert and Cornell Capa, Ernst Haas, Hansel Mieth, and Otto Hagel were among the immigrants whose vision fundamentally altered American visual culture.

Between 1941 and 1945, African, Puerto Rican, Mexican, Polish, Swedish, Jewish, and Filipino Americans, as well as Italian, Japanese, and German Americans served to protect ideals that government officials made no effort to recognize. While certain Germans and Italians were required to register as enemy aliens and were kept under surveillance during the war, special cruelty and insult were reserved for Japanese Americans. Forced to abandon homes, businesses, property, careers, and friendships, they were relocated to miserably overcrowded camps in desolate wilderness areas for more than two years. Those who didn't cooperate were jailed or

deported to Japan. Many young Japanese American men and women enlisted and bought back their unjustly tarnished reputations with their lives and exceptional battlefield heroism. In cities like Milwaukee, German Brown Shirts had marched publicly, prior to the war, in support of Hitler, yet no Germans were relocated to such camps. It took more than forty years for the U.S. government to admit to the egregious racism of the relocation policy.

After the war several hundred thousand "displaced persons" were allowed to come to the U.S. as refugees. Pressures of family reunification and the U.S. role in post-war European clean up and stabilization were the rationale for this, but hundreds of thousands more were denied entry. Nativists still feared floods of needy people. It remained clear that America had lost an important opportunity to match the battlefield heroism of her immigrant offspring in uniform, by the simple expedient of offering shelter to larger numbers of refugees when it was most needed.

In the early 1960s, the doors to America opened substantially. For the first time, large numbers of African, Asian and Latin American immigrants were invited to enter, provided they fell under categories of advanced skills. Nigerian Ph.D.s, East Indian M.D.s, Japanese mathematicians, and Brazilian physicists joined legions of refugees from communist regimes worldwide. Each was offered priority immigration, along with their spouses, children, and parents. The complexion of America was literally changing. With them came Buddha and the Tao, Ganesh and Xango, Allah and Ogun, and the Virgin of Guadalupe. They brought a thousand tongues, a million customs, and a rich spectrum of morality They took no longer to learn to pay taxes and vote Democrat/Republican than their predecessors did.

A teacher in Los Angeles regularly encounters Alieuts and Afghanis, Iranians and Irish, Japanese and Jamaicans, Mexicans and Moroccans, Poles and Pakistanis, Saudis and Scandinavians, Ugandans and Uruguayans, Venezuelans and Vietnamese. The same crude processes that created American citizens out of the polyglot masses one hundred years ago at Ellis Island work on the new crowds of Haitians, Cubans, Chinese, Hmong, Cambodians, Indians, Mexicans, Guatemalans, and eastern Europeans now arriving in New York, Miami, San Diego, or Wausau, Wisconsin.

Immigration issues have, in recent years, brought the U.S. to the brink of war and the invasion of Haiti. We have deployed thousands of officers along the Mexican border and collected thousands of Cubans floating on pitiful rafts off Florida's coast. We have apprehended citizens of ninety-three different countries illegally crossing the Mexico border at Tijuana. Hundreds of Chinese nationals have been rescued in California, New York and New Jersey from rotting ships and kidnapping rings. Even as every fault and failure of the United States is instantly televised around the globe, millions still

harbor the hyperbolic dream that led many of our ancestors to risk everything to get here. Those who risk everything to arrive here are not the cause of our problems; they may, in fact, be part of the solution.

It is impossible to know where the next wave will come from or what it will cost. But it is certain that we will all come to benefit from that wave and its progeny; their energy, initiative, intelligence and productivity will be utilized to create a stronger community fabric, with a more complex weave.

Intergroup animosities and rivalries have been with us always, often erupting in violence. In the 1850s, the anti-immigrant political party called the Know-Nothings had a short-lived but impressive success, electing six governors and dozens of state law makers. Such hatreds exist all over our world. America's strength is largely attributable to the extent to which these animosities have decreased and in many cases disappeared during our national history.

Nativists have always resisted new immigrants. The current anti-immigrant batch have sought to weigh all social concerns by their dollar cost. Statistics pile up on both sides of the issue but immigration cannot be reduced solely to cost factors. Just as educational costs are repaid by a better educated society decades in the future, and highway building is only worthwhile over the life of the road, the children and grandchildren of new immigrants and their contributions to our country must be considered as well. If it is too costly to

Americanize the newcomer, how has our immigrant country become a dominant world power?

Nativists have so twisted the issues that the public is now convinced that most of America's immigrants enter the country illegally. In fact only twenty-five percent do, according to the *Congressional Quarterly*.[8] The majority of the electorate believes that undocumented workers crossing the U.S./Mexico border make up the greatest percentage of illegals in the U.S. In fact, the largest number of illegals are visa-violators, who arrive legally on tourist visas and stay permanently. Legal immigration brings people generally better educated and earning more than the American population as a whole.[9]

It is often politically expedient to demonize illegal immigrants, to add more guards to the border, punish legal immigrants or citizen-children of undocumented workers, but we must not mistake these punitive actions for sound, long-term solutions to the nation's needs. The nation would benefit from a more subtle examination of the issues, and less inflammatory rhetoric. Through the centuries, America has forced some immigrants to come, seduced others, and repelled still others, but it has always used them as a vital force to build itself. The United States has needed immigrants as much as they have needed the United States. A recognition of the nation's needs must go far beyond immediate questions of costs. The simple fact remains that immigrants, with their

desire for a new beginning, with elevated hopes for their children, with their energies and their diverse perception of the broader world, are, and always have been, the best investment for the future of the nation and the best opportunity America has for a more realistic view of the world.

The photographs employed in this exhibition identify a spectrum of attitudes toward immigrants. Some are seen respectfully and some as intriguingly exotic, some as anonymous floods of threatening strangers, and some as bearers of odd gifts. Their common denominator is their determination to be here and to succeed here. Whether the days and years following these photographic exposures were rewarding or futile, it was the immigrants' effort that created the image of America which continues to draw the newest arrivals. ◄

1   Ronald Takaki, *Strangers from a Different Shore: A History of Asian Americans* (New York: Penguin, 1989), p. 79.
2   ibid, p. 99.
3   Ivan Chermayeff, Fred Waserman, and Mary J. Shapiro, *Ellis Island: An Illustrated History of the Immigration Experience* (New York: Macmillan Publishing Co., 1991), p. 56.
4   ibid, p. 192.
5. Carlos Fuentes, *The Buried Mirror: Reflections on Spain and the New World* (Boston, New York, and London: Houghton Mifflin Company, 1992), p. 342.
6   Thomas Kessner, "Immigration and the American Experience," in *The American Experience: Contemporary Immigrant Artists* (Philadelphia: The Balch Institute for Ethnic Studies and Independent Curators Inc.), pp. 27–28.
7   ibid, p. 29.
8   *Congressional Quarterly*, September 24, 1993, p. 845.
9   Alejandro Portes and Rubén Rumbaut: *Immigrant America: A Portrait* (Berkeley: University of California Press, 1990), p. 13. p. 15; p. 10.

Leonard Freed, Untitled, Wausau, Wisconsin, 1994, © Leonard Freed/Magnum Photos. Checklist #163

As immigrants have settled principally in large inner cities, they have filled neighborhoods often left nearly empty by the white flight to suburbs over the past forty years. They are also revitalizing the neighborhood schools with an influx of new students, and the attendant $5,000 or more in state funds that are spent annually on each student. In smaller communities, a sudden influx of immigrants can present many problems. This Hmong community is in a small midwestern city that is having difficulty accommodating the large numbers of new arrivals.

"YOU CANNOT SPILL A DROP OF AMERICAN BLOOD WITHOUT SPILLING THE BLOOD OF THE WHOLE WORLD.... OUR BLOOD IS AS THE FLOOD OF THE AMAZON, MADE UP OF A THOUSAND NOBLE CURRENTS, ALL POURING INTO ONE. WE ARE NOT A NATION, SO MUCH AS A WORLD." —HERMAN MELVILLE, *REDBURN: HIS FIRST VOYAGE*, 1849

BY VICKI GOLDBERG

The nineteenth century was consumed with a great urge to start over somewhere else—and that somewhere else was most often in America. From 1821 to 1924, when an American immigration act severely limited all immigration (especially from Asia), fifty-five million Europeans emigrated overseas; about thirty-three million of them came here (others came too, but not in numbers like these). Railroads and steamships having made travel easier, immigrants crossed the seas, built this country's railroads, and moved along the tracks to every corner of the land. Though people born here often felt their country was being overwhelmed by foreigners, the proportion of foreign-born people on this soil was quite stable, hovering between 13.2 percent and 14.7 percent every year between 1869 and 1920.[1]

During photography's early years, the camera recorded a lot of immigrant history without half trying. Up to the 1880s, while photographers created their trade and plied it, immigrants simply kept wandering into the frame. In avidly documenting the young republic, in diligently compiling archives—the century was awash with encyclopedic longings—in tracing the swift growth of urbanization and industrialization, photographers repeatedly, unavoidably, picked up the faces of new arrivals.

Immigrants were everywhere. In no time at all after arriving they were within camera view but not so easy to single out. Almost all of them were from northwestern Europe and Great Britain, as earlier immigrants had been, and those from urban centers already wore similar clothes. Immediately, and without even thinking about it, they set about fashioning the new nation. For half a century, photographers did not consider the new arrivals a cause. Illustrated newspapers published articles on immigration as early as the 1850s, but their engravings do not claim to be from photographs. Not till close to 1890, when the newcomers were a matter of national concern and photography an inseparable element of the news, did photographers put immigration itself into their programs as a separate and important subject. Until then, most photographs of immigrants were essentially incidental to other photographic categories.

Successful immigrants, for example, commissioned studio portraits from the beginning, just as everyone else did. Their money entitled them to the same kind of serious and respect-

David McNew, *U.S. Coast Guard man throws a blanket to Chinese boat people,* 1993. © 1995 David McNew. Checklist #200

Since the early 1990s, Chinese people without documents have attempted to reach the U.S. in aging and rusted, barely seaworthy ships. Their travel is organized by unscrupulous smuggling rings, which create exorbitant profits both by charging large sums for transportation, and by holding the passengers captive in "safe houses" in the United States until their families in China pay a ransom to release them. The immigrants then drift into the twilight world of exploitation in illegal sweatshops or sub-minimum-wage restaurant work. This ship was intercepted off the Mexican coast on its way to California. It was towed to Ensenada, Mexico. Its passengers were briefly held in Mexico and the majority were returned to China.

Andreas Larsen Dahl, *Rev. John A. Ottesen house and family, Utica Township, Dane County, Wisconsin,* 1874, printed later. Checklist #26

This proud and sober family poses at tea in front of their home. The Norwegian flag illustrates their continuing devotion to their country of origin.

ful images that long-time inhabitants took home (some immigrants set up their own studios to record their own kind). Or the newcomers commissioned pictures of themselves with their houses, their property, their businesses—status pictures, ownership pictures, we-made-it pictures, highly significant for a new nation that had already embraced work and success as national characteristics. Westering migrants and long-term inhabitants commissioned ownership

pictures too; they were an integral part of the photographic record of American urban growth.[2]

Such property portraits from the Midwest and the West, often graced with fine land that had been wrested from native peoples, have the stiffness and charm of folk art. They were taken outdoors, probably at least as much for the light conditions as the view of the building and property. Though carefully staged, they evidently aim for the studied informality of a Gainsborough conversation piece. Often the families cart outside domestic exhibits of their success: a good chair, a tea table, a painting. A farm family in Nebraska displays their enterprise and culture: their mule, pigs, cows, farm implements—and their pump organ.

Surely some of these pictures traveled back to Europe to say the trip was worth it, life is good here, your new grandchildren are doing well, perhaps you should come too. . . . In this great era of travel, photographs became major links with people one might never see again, even a peculiar kind of substitute for family; pictures of immigrants must have been as important to those who stayed behind as to those who commissioned a record of what they had become.

Their foreign names indicate where immigrant store owners were from, but sometimes too the proprietors advertised their American-ness with a flag or a wealth of bunting. The immigrant automatically takes out a dual citizenship of the mind. Our own century is well supplied with photographs of Italian American, Cuban American and other clubs that sport two flags side by side, as well as pictures of nation-day celebrations that insist on allegiance to this country, like the photograph of young Norwegian women in 1929 coquettishly wrapping themselves in the American flag. Immigrant ownership pictures today still feature retail stores, but now the pictures are usually taken indoors, where distinctive goods and decor make identifications that last names once supplied.

American dedication to work was immediately evident to nineteenth century observers—foreign commentators often remarked on it—and a country intent on defining itself naturally recorded its workers. The U.S. recruited labor from abroad to power its rapid industrialization; immigrants were essential to the definition of America as a mighty nation.[3]

Pictures of immigrants at work might amount to chattel records: from the seventeenth century on, men had come here as indentured workers who were little better off than slaves. A daguerreotype of a European apparently overseeing a group of Chinese miners might be such a story, told in the camera's noncommittal documentary tone.

The camera had other tones at its disposal, and labor had other conditions. Manual workers often look heroically confident—photography is good at admiration. In more ostensibly neutral images, laborers were lined up across the picture plane or arrayed in groups. Similar compositions turn up in industrializing countries around the world. No doubt the

large group pictures were records of a businessman's success: my factory, my employees, and, on occasion, my strikebreakers. Once the twentieth century arrived, Lewis Hine and later photographers like Russell Lee and Gordon Parks would speak specifically to the multicultural composition of the labor pool, the ways that physical labor compels integration.

By the time Ellis Island opened in 1892 and Angel Island in 1910, primary immigration shifted, now coming principally from southeastern Europe. The number of arrivals swelled so precipitously that urban existence radically and visibly changed, and the camera moved in purposefully to record the shift. At just the right moment, photography and techniques of reproduction became capable of documenting the news for a mass audience with a compelling interest in the subject.

History had handed photography a new category: arrival pictures (departure pictures, taken at major ports across the Atlantic, had been popular among painters and photographers for some years. The painter Ford Maddox Brown, in *The Last of England* [1852–55], expressed the difficulty and melancholy of sailing out of one's homeland into the unknown). Photographs of people on boats and docks in American harbors were news; they fed curiosity and the need to understand momentous change. Photographs of medical and legal inspections at Ellis and Angel Islands early in the century might have been for government records (which would mean that almost no one saw them)

Unknown artist, *SE corner of Division & Noble; headquarters of the Kosciusko Guards*, c. 1910s. Checklist #94

The patriotism of the newly-arrived is generally more enthusiastic than that of the second, third, or fourth generation citizen.

or could have been journalistic assignments—it would be worth knowing if they were published, and in what context.

New immigrants, if visibly different either in costume or complexion, were tinged with an exoticism that made for saleable images. Genre pictures, coming from a long tradition in both painting and photography, combined the exotic and the winsome. Chinese vendors posed before painted, orientalizing backdrops; women in babushkas were properly shy and unassuming in the studio.

The Chinese obligingly looked distinctly different. From 1896 to 1906, Arnold Genthe photographed in San

W. F. Song Studio, Untitled (studio portrait of a Chinese woman), San Francisco, c. 1890. Checklist #37

This lovely, traditional western portrait motif was adopted by Chinese photographer Song. Thirty years earlier, identical poses were used by European photographers traveling in China.

Francisco's Chinatown, carefully removing any evidence of westerners or westernization from his frames. These pictures insisted on, even created, difference and separateness. Postcards of Chinese in traditional dress and guidebooks to New York's and San Francisco's Chinatowns also touted the lure of Asia to the tourist on his own home ground; someone could always find a way to make money off the Chinese.

Thus could immigrants be turned into objects by photographers and cameras, which defined them not merely as Other but as commodities, with limited control over their lives and none over their images. The Chinese had some control in the beginning. They first came here voluntarily in the California gold rush and staked out their own claims;[4] respectful early portraits, even daguerreotypes, exist and were probably commissioned by the sitters. But by the time Eadweard Muybridge, a British immigrant himself, took a picture of such a prospector, he was confident enough of his superior insider's position and of a widely intolerant audience to caption his photograph "the heathen Chinee" after a well-known poem by Stephen Crane.

Genthe was not much more respectful of the needs and desires of his Chinese subjects. Some covered their faces when they saw him, which he assumed was a superstitious reaction, so he cleverly concealed his camera. Maxine Hong Kingston says that, in fact, many were illegal immigrants, fearful of being identified and deported.[5]

Immigrants just off the boat, dressed in their very foreign best in hopes of passing inspection for the new land, were surveyed by Augustus Sherman, who worked as a clerk and inspector at Ellis Island beginning in 1892. An amateur, he took what amounted to genre pictures, rather like portraits of American Indians at the time.

The era's curiosity about "exotic" and disappearing cultures, spiked by photographs that fostered armchair tourism, made "native villages" at worlds' fairs highly popular. Photographs reinforced the nineteenth century colonial notion that people who were different enough were both quaint and inferior. Also, as the century progressed, anthropology was organized on a scientific basis, as were national and institutional record keeping; the camera played a major role in a kind of worldwide anthropological preservation project.

Sherman's pictures were not shown or published; today they and other pictures of arriving foreigners have a peculiar shine of ambivalence. No matter how particular the newcomers' dress and hair arrangements and, in some cases, race, their "exoticism" implies the potential of its own erasure. Racial differences are not, of course, readily eradicated, and there never was a melting pot. Some immigrants then and now clung to their separate traditions, but most came for a new life, and it was generally accepted then that assimilation was a prerequisite for success. Gradually, most new arrivals shed their distinguishing marks. It is hard to imagine the splendid, warrior-like group of Ethiopians at Ellis Island still cloaked and carrying shields five years later.

Sometimes a photograph captures the moment of transition, another new subject: children at Ellis Island with American flags stuck in their hands; a group of Chinese boys at home, some wearing oriental robes, others western clothing. Sometimes the modern, western world asserts itself, as when contemporary Buddhist monks sit on the floor in a Bronx apartment with a telephone and electronic gadgets. Recent photography picks up on the countertrend, always present, now fervently embraced: the preservation of some elements and rituals of the past. The old and the new co-exist in the fluid balance, caught by the camera in the fleeting present: Japanese American children wear paper samurai helmets, nation-day parades temporarily restore native costumes no longer worn much even in the country where they originated.

Religions perform major preservative functions, ensuring continuities of belief, rites, the familiar language of chants, prayers, and stories, the trusted sameness of things: priestly garments, icons, aids to worship. Photographs of priests, rituals, and congregants emphasize both their strangeness and their spirituality, reminding wary viewers that the new immigrants are God-fearing people, at least in their own ways.

Departure, arrival and transition pictures are with us still. Departures have periodically become news again—at the borders of Rwanda

and Zaire, on the beaches of Cuba. Arrival pictures, once brimful of the future (at least to the people in them) have now taken on an air of desperation, partly because so many immigrants are or claim to be refugees.

Haitians in tiny, makeshift boats and Mexicans running across highways may reach the other side without being killed, but what waits for them here might be only a blanket in a field, erratic and low-wage jobs, detention or deportation. In our image-conscious and cynical era, the post-arrival pictures of detention camps no longer dare the propaganda stickiness of Japanese American women happily stitching up American flags in World War II internment camps. Today, the images tend to be sulky and rough and redolent of empty days.

Mel Rosenthal, *A Buddhist Monastery, Marion Avenue, the Bronx, September, 1985,* © 1995 Mel Rosenthal. Checklist #139

This area of the Bronx is a relocation center for Vietnamese people. There are now more than 8,000 Vietnamese in the neighborhood. By 1985, when this photograph was taken, there were 643,000 Vietnamese people residing in the U.S.

All immigrants lose some of their original and distinctive characteristics in their frictive contact with their new country. All assimilate to a degree and, regardless of their capacity for change, none can do so absolutely. The change process is slow as customs, appearance, traditions, accents, and occupations all adapt to the here-and-now. A prayer service on the floor of a Bronx apartment can be like—but not exactly like— a similar practice in Vietnam.

Walter Michot, *Cuban rafters in open sea*, 1994. © 1994
Walter Michot, *The Miami Herald*. Checklist #202

*Cuban refugees to the United States in
1994 traveled on virtually anything that
floated. The ninety mile journey through
often very rough water is potentially deadly,
but hundreds of such rafts made the crossing. They were regularly intercepted by
coast guard vessels and taken to processing
centers in Guantanamo Bay on the island
of Cuba.*

If arrival and transition photographs were by-products of immigration, immigrants were crucial to
two other new photographic subjects:
poverty and social reform. Until the
social reform movement gathered
strength in the later nineteenth century, Americans were not prepared to
see the poor depicted realistically
(rather than charmingly, picturesque-
ly) and to be concerned about their

plight. Probably the first to think of
documenting immigrant life and
experience as independent subjects
was Jacob Riis, an immigrant himself, who limned the conditions in
New York tenements beginning in
1887 and encountered immigrants
everywhere he looked. Lewis Hine's
view was more longitudinal and historical: he began photographing at
Ellis Island in 1904 at the outset of
a career of social concern. Later, he
followed some of the new arrivals
into their jobs and homes in pursuit
of an overall picture of American life
and labor.

Around the turn of the century,
photographers recording the social
reform movement duly noted efforts
to assist the new immigrants and
turn them into good Americans. Religious institutions mobilized to bring
the newcomers into the fold: volunteers handed out Bibles at Ellis

Island, Christian societies founded
orphanages, took in rescued slave
girls, organized classes and orches-
tras, groups and Sunday schools.

The photographic records of
social workers and reformers teach-
ing foreigners how to care for their
babies, speak English and learn other
skills for their new lives clearly were
not made for the immigrants themselves. They look rather like news-
worthy propaganda for the societies
whose good—and sometime vital—
works they advertise. A smartly
dressed New York woman counsels a
poor immigrant mother, and citizens
who conform in every detail of out-
ward appearance shepherd flocks of
children or adults who have not yet
learned to (or wished to, or been able
to) look "American."

Because immigration into this
nation of immigrants has been so
controversial, photographers focus-
ing on the newly arrived have always
been in a delicate position; their
intentions and stance might make a
difference in public opinion. For
most of the nineteenth century, when
photography did not engage in many
polemical crusades, virulent anti-
immigrant feelings were more likely
to be expressed by cartoonists. When
Riis set out to correct hideous living
conditions, he had a stake in pictur-
ing impoverished immigrants as bald-
ly as possible, whereas Hine was
predisposed to portray the newcomers sympathetically (the popularity of
his pictures of Madonna-like mothers
and children and lovely, vulnerable
young women has probably exagger-
ated the common notion of how

many women came to America when immigration was still predominantly male).

The outpouring of photographs on the subject today, encouraged by the most image-dependent communications era in history, reflects acrimonious debates about borders, employment, and identity. Enormous increases in migrations the world over have prompted unease everywhere, and economic troubles in this country have always fed anti-immigrant sentiment. The photographic response ranges across the documentary spectrum. Few photographers would profess to be anti-immigrant, but hard-hitting photojournalistic traditions encourage scathing pictures of overcrowding, wretchedness, violence. Some of the tougher photographs are meant to elicit concern, though the eye of certain beholders will not read them that way. Some are arguably images of success—people who live in good-enough housing, wear intact clothing, and are probably better off than they were before coming to America—but they generate an atmosphere of sullenness and hostility that amounts to a threat.

Many of the subjects are still exotic, some now willfully so, exalting their differences. Many of the images are apostles of good will, presenting likeable, cheerful people in family units, workers, strivers, dreamers, as if to say: this is the new America; this is a good place to be.

Immigrants' public images have been largely in someone else's hands, and for the most part still are. Journalistic and documentary photographs are generally taken by people with more access to the media than their subjects have. Illegal crossings, rescue at sea, detention are not moments proudly recorded for one's grandchildren, and even people in gentler circumstances are still strangers viewed from the outside with an agenda that might not match their own. But immigrants with only a little money can afford a camera, and they too have the common, modern desire to record their families and rites of passage. An exhibition of their family albums would doubtless tell us something these photographs do not.

Ironically, photography has unwittingly played a larger role in immigration than all its programs of documenting, commodifying and pleading the cause of the new arrivals ever accomplished: it has helped to swell the tide of immigrants. Still photography and its derivative movie and video forms have doubtless pulled people to these shores. In the last century, photographs of successful immigrants mailed back home probably encouraged others to follow. But in the twentieth century, widely distributed American movies, then television and satellite relay, spread across the globe the image of American economic success and abundant consumer goods, honing the dissatisfactions of upwardly mobile people everywhere, presenting them with images of an American candy store of opportunities.

From the lowest classes to professional doctors and lawyers, people in many lands look at our photo-essays, feature films and commercials, our soaps and our sitcoms, and see representations of better lives than they can make at home. Images lodge in their minds like promises, and thousands upon thousands, instructed by the camera, pack their belongings, kiss their relatives goodbye, and cross oceans, borders and barricades to put themselves into the American picture. ◄

1   Roger Daniels, *Coming to America: A History of Immigration and Ethnicity in American Life* (New York: Harper Collins, 1990), pp. 23, 25.
2   Peter B. Hales, *Silver Cities: The Photography of American Urbanization, 1839–1915* (Philadelphia: Temple University Press, 1984), pp. 25–26.
3   On labor, see Richard Rudisill, *Mirror Image: The Influence of the Daguerreotype on American Society* (Albuquerque: University of New Mexico Press, 1971), Chapter 1. On the need for laborers, see Alejandro Portes and Rubén G. Rumbaut, *Immigrant America: A Portrait* (Berkeley: University of California Press, 1990), p. 13.
4   Ronald Takaki, *Strangers from a Different Shore: A History of Asian Americans* (New York: Penguin, 1989), p. 36.
5   Maxine Hong Kingston, *American Heritage*, December, 1978.

James Wallace Black, *Carl Schurz, Secretary of Interior,* c. 1860s. Checklist #9

James Wallace Black, *Louis Agassiz, 1807–1873, Swiss-born American Naturalist,* c. 1860s. Checklist #8

By the time photography became democratically available to the American public (mid-1840s), much of the social and political structure of the nation had been well developed. Huge immigration waves, principally of western Europeans and British subjects, arrived long before photographic documentation was possible. Thus, cities, farms, universities, courts, and businesses were well populated by immigrants or their great-great-grandchildren before the technology to produce the first photographs was available in America. A few representatives, in this case European immigrants themselves, will stand for these large flows of productive arrivals and their progeny.

Napolean Sarony, *Photographer, self-portrait,* c. 1860s. Checklist #6

Unknown artist, Untitled (John Hillers, photographer, on right), c. 1860s. Checklist #7

400,000 NEW ACRES.

HOME OF OLE SWENSON, MARSHALL CO., MINNESOTA.

THE above is engraved from a photograph of the home of Ole Swenson, as taken in December last. It is produced here as a real example of what can be done by an honest, industrious, frugal, intelligent farmer and his wife, if they try. See their all on forty acres of land bought on time in 1882. Again, see them after six years on the same 40, with 120 more added to it, after working, and selling butter, eggs, poultry, hogs, cattle, horses, wheat, oats, and barley, and devoting the proceeds to buying and making a home.

—— THE ——

ST. PAUL, MINNEAPOLIS
& MANITOBA R'y Co.

Has recently obtained Deeds from the Government for

—⇥ 400,000 ACRES ⇤—

more just such land, and is offering it for sale to actual settlers on terms such as have enabled Swenson to make himself and frugal wife comfortable as long as they live.

Now that Oklahoma has been found to be the remains of an old brick yard, and a place without water or bread, would it not be well to seek the land where the best of wheat, oats and barley are produced; where the best wool can be grown, and where the fattest cattle and hogs can be found and the strongest horses can be grown, and where every creature from child to chicken is healthy? Then write for free maps and information to

J. BOOKWALTER,
Land Commissioner,
ST. PAUL, MINN.

PIONEER PRESS, ST. PAUL, MINN.

Unknown artist, *400,000 New Acres* (broadside, issued by St. Paul, Minneapolis and Manitoba Realty Company), c. 1888. Checklist #19

This nearly breathless, hard-sell text does everything short of identifying Minnesota as Eden. The couple referred to is a nineteenth century description of model immigrants. Their fine choice, hard work, and sound financial controls have produced the American Dream. No mention is made of the fact that ca. ten years earlier, the land was still in the hands of its original native tribes. In 1862, eight hundred settlers in the Upper Minnesota River Valley were killed by Sioux Chief Little Crow and his warriors when the U.S. government failed to live up to its promises to the Sioux Nation. By 1876, the Sioux were still a powerful enough force in their neighboring Dakota Territory that they destroyed General Custer and his troops at Little Big Horn. Farmland was being occupied at the owner's own risk.

Facing page: **Solomon D. Butcher,** Untitled (the Hilton family, immigrants from England, on their homestead near Weissert, Custer County, Nebraska), c. 1889. Checklist #36

The Nebraska farmer from England sits in his farmyard with his family and the utensils of his new life: buckboard, plow, animals, and pump organ. The high vantage point indicates that the photographer was on the roof of the home, allowing a better view of the expansive yard and corral. The focus is on the immensity that this family has under its control. The land and its productivity are paramount, but the people (who don't seem to be overburdened), are well dressed and ready for music. Families of pigs, cows, and donkeys lounge similarly nearby with visual references to fertility and increase. This bearded Noah has survived his journey over the flood and begun to be fruitful in the "new world." The year is 1889 in Custer County, Nebraska, a mere thirteen years after this area's namesake was destroyed at the Little Big Horn. The blood of native peoples and new Americans fertilized the rich prairie soil for the benefit of newcomers.

The photographer, Solomon Butcher (1856–1927) had Custer County's first portrait studio. He principally recorded families and the details of their lives. More than portraits, his images capture the pioneer spirit at a time of transition on the plains.

The Irish were the most rural Europeans, and they became the most urban Americans. They principally settled in their ports of arrival: New York, Boston, Philadelphia, and Chicago—the terminus of the Western railroad. By the 1860s they were evident in a few western areas like Kansas. Police work was a typical Irish occupation.

Andreas Larsen Dalen (1844–1923) spent his first twenty-four years working a poor rugged farm in Norway with his father. His older brother left Norway for Wisconsin, and upon their father's death the farm passed to Andreas. Within a year, he sold the farm and left Norway, arriving in Wisconsin to join his brother on May 14, 1869.

Quickly becoming an ambitious new American, Dalen changed his last name to Dahl, and in the census of 1870 he reported his profession as "daguerrian artist." It is not known if he brought his photographic skills with him from Norway, or if he picked them up in Wisconsin. There was no doubt, however, that he was never destined to be a simple country photographer. Dahl considered himself an artist and approached his medium with creativity and persistence.

Andreas Larsen Dahl, *Siri Rustebakke, center, with daughters and daughter-in-law, Town of Black Earth, Wisconsin*, c. 1873/ printed later. Checklist #23

Taking his photography further than the typical landscape photographs of the day, Dahl convinced otherwise conservative farmers and townspeople to haul their parlors out into their front yards—tables, chairs, pianos, and all. Dahl traveled from the first thaw of spring through to the first frost of fall taking pictures, and spent the winter making prints he hoped to sell the following season.

In 1879, at the age of thirty-five, Dahl was stricken with a terrible fever, and swore if he survived he would devote his life to God. At an age when most nineteenth century men had been long-established in their careers, Dahl entered the Norwegian Evangelical Lutheran Seminary in Madison. Ordained in 1883, Dahl worked as a minister in Wisconsin for the next forty-four years.

850—The "Heathen Chinee" with pick and rocker.

Eadweard J. Muybridge, *The 'Heathen Chinee' with pick and rocker*, 1868–1872. Checklist #13

In China, during the 1840s and 1850s, teenagers—and often children—were captured on the streets and from their homes and sold into contract labor in America. These "shanghaied" unfortunates never returned to their families, were sequestered in squalid mining camps and "Chinatowns," and denied every freedom according to U.S. law. Thousands of other young Chinese people expected to sojourn in America for a number of years to work, save, and return to a better life in China. Their segregation from American opportunity regularly drew them into poverty, disillusionment, and immobility; they could not dwell in most towns, and they were forbidden by law to bring their wives and families, or to marry non-Chinese. As their expenses were lower than those of others, they had no choice but to survive on the poorest income.

William Shew, *Gold Mining with Chinese Workers*, c. 1850. Checklist #5

Chinese miners in California's gold country eventually obtained rights to small claims found to be unprofitable by other miners. In 1852, the California legislature enacted a tax on foreign miners— principally against Chinese and Mexicans. The $3-per-month tax on any miner who did not wish to become a citizen dovetailed nicely with previous federal legislation that denied citizenship to any non- white. A Civil Rights Act of 1870 ended this tax, but not before it had raised $5 million from Chinese miners, representing one-quarter to one-half of all state revenue during that period.

Source: Charles J. McClain, Jr., "The Chinese Struggle for Civil Rights in Nineteenth Century America: The First Phase, 1850–1870," *California Law Review*, vol. 72, (1984), pp. 544, 555.

Alfred A. Hart, *Railroad construction at Secrettown, Sierra Nevada*, c. 1868. Checklist #17

As Chinese miners were violently pushed out of the gold fields, their services were desired to build the transcontinental railroad. More than twelve thousand of them composed 90 percent of the work force of the Central Pacific Railroad. The construction of the Central Pacific Railroad was a Chinese achievement. "The Chinese workers were," in one observer's description, "a great army laying siege to Nature in her strongest citadel. The rugged mountains looked like stupendous anthills. They swarmed with Celestials, shoveling, wheeling, carting, drilling and blasting rocks and earth . . . managers forced the Chinese laborers to work through the winter of 1866. Snow drifts, over sixty feet tall, covered construction operations. The workers lived and worked in tunnels under the snow, with shafts for air and lanterns for light."

Source: Ronald Takaki, *A Different Mirror: A History of Multi-Cultural America*, 1993.

Keller, *"First Blow at the Chinese Question"*, 1877. Checklist #31

Chinese people developed enclaves throughout the West in mining and railroad areas. They were segregated, mistrusted, and feared. As they were never paid equally with white workers, and were in some demand by employers, they were feared by labor organizations. In 1869, the railroad completed, thousands left for San Francisco, where the Chinese community provided one-half of the city's labor force. They worked principally in shoe, cigar, and woolen manufacturing, and in the sweat shops of the sewing trades.

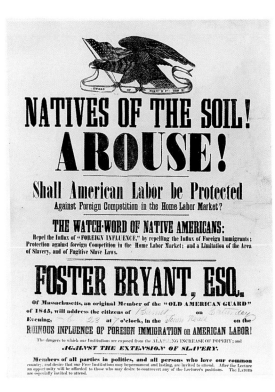

Unknown artist, *'Beware of Foreign Influence!'*, 1850. Checklist #10

Labor unions have feared the competition of new arrivals who were willing to undercut prevailing wages to get a foothold in America. Capitalizing on their discrimination, employers found the Chinese to be a seductive alternative to increasingly organized and militant white laborers.

The anti-immigrant chorus has always been with us, but is, in fact, a mixture of racist voices momentarily harmonizing with workers who feel their livelihood is threatened, as well as with employers interested in cheap productivity. The politician, who owes nothing to immigrant workers (who are not citizens and, therefore, have no franchise to vote), directs the whole performance, hoping for a large and cheering audience.

T. Thulstrup, after C. A. Booth, *The Massacre of the Chinese at Rock Springs, Wyoming*, c. 1885. Checklist #18

The Rock Springs Massacre is a famous example of the explosive racial hatred manifested toward Chinese people in the rural west. In this eruption, fifteen Chinese workers were killed. Other Chinese enclaves were simply uprooted and the people forcibly placed on trains heading out of the area.

Arnold Genthe, *Street of the Gamblers, Chinatown, San Francisco*, c. 1900. Checklist #46

As evidenced by the traditional papier-mâché garlands hanging above the doorway on the building to the right, this photograph was taken around New Year's when seasonal workers were laid off, inundating Chinatown streets with thousands of idle workers. Their cotton tunic tops and cloth shoes are Chinese, but the pants and felt homburg-style hats are strictly Western. Genthe's title, "The Street of the Gamblers" is accurate insofar as Ross Alley had many gambling rooms, but it unfairly ascribes a sinister quality to these men.

Source: *Genthe's Photographs of San Francisco's Old Chinatown,* Photographs by Arnold Genthe, Selection and Text by John Kuo Wei Tchen, p. 63, plate 47.

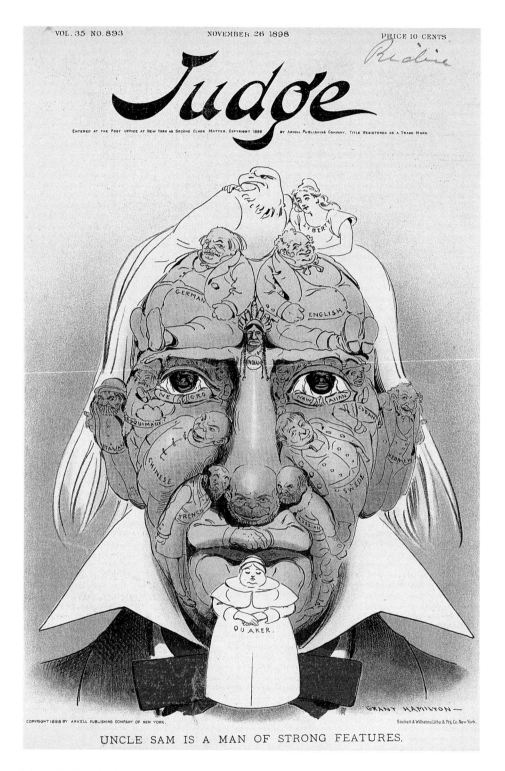

Grant Hamilton, *"Uncle Sam is a Man of Strong Features,"* 1898. Checklist #50

Through the use of what today would be considered objectionable caricatures, Grant Hamilton identifies America's greatest strength.

Unknown artist, *Chinatown, New York City, New Year, January 30, 1911,* printed later. Checklist #88

Clothing is an important index of adopting American culture. Three of these boys have Americanized their wardrobes and two have not. It has usually been the men and children who have discarded their "foreign" clothing first because of their need to interface with the new culture in work or school. Women who stayed home were generally able to change their styles of clothing more slowly. There have been exceptions among Irish and Jewish immigrant women, as well as various others, who have strongly insisted on Americanizing their appearance. Immigrant children are sometimes embarrassed by their parents' "old country" clothing, customs, and language.

F. Benjamin Johnston, Untitled (women and children sitting on deck of *S.S. Amsterdam*), c. 1897. Checklist #49

Steamships changed the demographics of immigration. The earlier English, German, and Dutch immigrants of northern and western Europe were replaced by Russian Jews, Italians, Turks, and others from eastern and southern Europe. Huge, fast, and inexpensive, the steamships allowed large numbers of poorer people to move to the U.S.

Augustus Sherman, *Women from Guadeloupe, French West Indies, at Ellis Island after arrival on* S.S. Korona, 1911.
Checklist #61

There is evident pride and dignity in the bearing of these well-attired and proud-standing Caribbean women. The photograph identifies them as free, self-possessed, and confident. It would not take long for them to realize that just such postures and dignity would irritate some Americans who never expected Blacks of any origin to enjoy American prosperity. The bearing that was useful in Guadeloupe might be a liability in St. Louis. In spite of racism and minimal opportunity, many Blacks who came by their own choice have, in fact, found economic success.

Frederick Burr Opper, *"Castle Garden Emigrant-Catchers,"* c. 1882. Checklist #41

Castle Garden, located at the southern tip of Manhattan, was the nation's first receiving station for immigrants. It opened in 1855 and operated for thirty-seven years, during which time it processed nine million immigrants. By 1890, Castle Garden's facilities and procedures were overrun by the huge numbers of arrivals. Ellis Island, in upper New York Bay near the New Jersey shore, was selected as the site of a much larger processing center.

Upon emerging from Castle Garden into lower Manhattan, immigrants often became prey to hustlers and con-men who fed on their naïveté. This cartoon identifies the problems of the new arrivals.

CASTLE GARDEN EMIGRANT-CATCHERS.

Augustus Sherman, *"John D. Third and family, natives of Scotland,* S.S. Caledonia, *September 17, 1905. Went to friend, John Fleming, Anniston, Alabama,"* printed later. Checklist #54

Little is known about Augustus Sherman's early life. He was born in Pennsylvania in the late 1850s and moved to New York at the age of twenty-two. His first job at Ellis Island was registering immigrants as they entered the United States. In 1921, Sherman was promoted to the prestigious post of private secretary to the Commissioner of Immigration, where he remained until his death in 1925. From these two positions at Ellis Island, Sherman found a wealth of subject matter to photograph.

The photographs Sherman took of immigrants between 1892 and 1925 serve as one of the most substantial photographic records of that period of mass immigration. Photographic documentation was not a requirement upon entrance to the United States. Therefore Sherman's photographs are particularly significant.

Unknown artist, *African immigrants, Ellis Island*, c. 1910, printed later. Checklist #86

These immigrants numbered among the numerous groups that arrived from Africa in the early twentieth century. This group came from what is now Ethiopia, then known as Abyssinia.

Unknown artist, *Hungarian immigrant family, Ellis Island*, c. 1900, printed later. Checklist #66

Immigrants made every effort to present themselves in their best light at Ellis Island. Often decked out in their native finery, they wanted to be seen as healthy and respectful, upstanding and proud. This industrious mother clearly obtained a bolt of fabric to make clothing for all her children to wear for their arrival in America.

Lewis Hine, *Albanian Woman, Ellis Island*, c. 1905. Checklist #75

The upheaval produced by leaving one country, one culture, one language, and one value system for another suggests that, for the rest of her life, the immigrant will be judged by values and standards imperfectly understood. She will forever speak an accented language and eternally judge one reality by a receding and fading past. The immigrant may later come to realize that, rather than subscribing to two national identities, she often has none.

Augustus Sherman, Untitled (two Dutch children at Ellis Island), c. 1910. Checklist #56

Among the earliest, largest, and most successful groups, the Dutch established New Amsterdam (New York) and produced many of the nation's prominent business and political leaders. Between 1850 and 1950, nearly one million immigrants came to the U.S. from The Netherlands.

Augustus Sherman, Untitled (three Dutch Women at Ellis Island), c. 1910. Checklist #62

Ellis Island was a show place for costumes from many nationalities. It was generally only a matter of days before the most extreme manifestations of "foreign" dress were put aside in favor of more "American" clothing.

Important ceremonial occasions prompt individuals to retrieve their finest traditional garments. Weddings, christenings, bar mitzvahs, holidays, and funerals—even several generations after immigration—may employ native garments originally worn by ancestors.

Augustus Sherman, *Children's Playground, Ellis Island Roof Garden*, c. 1910, printed later. Checklist #53

Most people stayed on Ellis Island no more than four hours. Those who were detained for further examination, who awaited word from sponsors, or who were being treated in the infirmary, were allowed fresh air and exercise, as well as early indoctrination in American customs, on the roof of the main building.

Lewis Hine, *Joys and Sorrows at Ellis Island*, c. 1905. Checklist #76

Lewis Hine's image elegantly encapsulates the powerful emotions associated with leaving one country and one life, and beginning another.

Lewis Hine. *Italian Girl at Ellis Island Finds her First Penny.* 1926. Checklist #79

One of Lewis Hine's most touching photographs illustrates with poignancy a young Italian girl with her first penny. While the event is no doubt factual, it points to the capacity of a photograph to elicit an emotional understanding of the profundity of the immigration experience. This little girl is just beginning life as an American. Her innocence and earnestness stand—in Hine's vision—as the identifiers of all hardworking immigrants. She could be the ultimate Ellis Island "poster child."

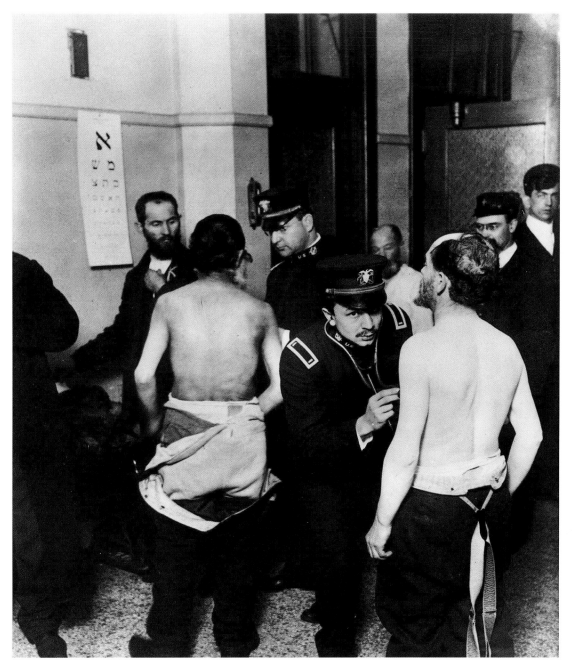

Unknown artist, *Physical examination, Ellis Island*, c. 1895. Checklist #48

Arriving in America with a physical disorder could result in weeks or months of detention on Ellis Island, or deportation. Not only serious illnesses could cause exclusion. Physical anomalies, mental retardation, blindness, deafness, as well as general weakness and moral deficiencies, could result in non-admission. Circuses and side shows could sponsor the true anomalies for quick passage off the island.

The examination for trachoma was one of the most feared trials of all. If the disease was found, the unfortunate individual was required to return to his/her place of origin by the next departing ship. It was common for a parent and child to be forever separated by this exam.

J. H. Adams, *"Contract Laborers to be Deported," Regulation of Immigration at the Port of Entry, New York City,* 1900. © 1973 Carpenter Center for the Visual Arts, Harvard University. Checklist #70

As frightening as the trip to the New World might have been, the immigrant's greatest fear was of not being admitted. One might be forced to return to an uncertain future if one was seen as morally unfit, unemployable, an unaccompanied woman with no sponsor or support, of low intelligence, or in poor health.

J. H. Adams, *"Saved at the Last Moment (Through an Appeal, the Order to Deport was Revoked)," Port of Entry, New York City,* 1900. © 1973 Carpenter Center for the Visual Arts, Harvard University. Checklist #71

At best, only a short appeals process was available to a rejected, would-be immigrant. Very few rejections were overturned. This man's good fortune was not lost on him.

Jacob A. Riis, *"Ready for Sabbath Eve in a Coal cellar," A cobbler in Ludlow Street*, c. 1895, printed later. Checklist #44

Even the poorest of the poor in the Jewish community would save enough each week to enjoy the Sabbath with a loaf of Challah (egg bread). Jacob Riis clearly engaged the trust of the lowest classes in order to photograph them. He was, himself, a Scandinavian immigrant who had experienced homelessness and poverty.

Jacob A. Riis, *Home of an Italian Ragpicker, Jersey Street*, c. 1894, printed later. Checklist #42

Young Italian men came in huge numbers without their wives and children, as sojourners, to work for several years, save some money, and return to their families in Italy. Nearly half of them did, in fact, return home. Others, who had begun to establish themselves, sent for relatives to join them and became American citizens. They settled principally in their ports of landing— Boston, New York, Philadelphia, and the major rail terminus, Chicago.

Lewis Hine, *Steelworkers at Russian boarding house, Homestead, Pennsylvania*, c. 1907. Checklist #78

The prospect of employment is now, as it has always been, the principal lure for immigrants. Organized labor has generally resisted immigration because many immigrants willingly work cheaply and with few protections, driving wages and benefits down. It has been common for employers to play one immigrant group off against another to lower wages further. The undocumented worker is the easiest to intimidate, as he/she has no legal or union protections. These Russian steelworkers were seen by Lewis Hine as powerful, proud and earnest.

Lewis Hine was one of the best of the documentary photographers whose work was used by politicians and the press to pass laws against child labor. Throughout his career he cast a strong photographic light on the lives of the underclass.

Unknown artist, *Finnish Lumber Crew, Wolf River, Wisconsin*, 1904. Checklist #80

Rural Scandinavians gravitated to Wisconsin and Minnesota—areas that were remarkably similar to their old countries' homes. They brought useful knowledge and skill to the U.S. and quickly established their communities. Long before mechanized clear-cutting of forests, these lumbermen cleared much of the farmland in the Upper Midwest. This heroic image is a typical illustration of the conquest of a harsh nature by persistence and a strong arm.

Boulanger et Frères, Untitled (coal & ice workers, mostly French Canadians, in Manchester, New Hampshire), c. 1900, printed later. Checklist #67

French Protestants were ejected from Catholic France in 1685. Known as Huguenots, some came to the U.S. and others settled in eastern Canada. Paul Revere was a well-known Huguenot. Of those settling in the United States, many lived in Louisiana and in the state of Maine. Today, Lewiston, Maine is often referred to as the largest French speaking city in the United States.

Unknown artist, *A General Strike is Declared in the Clothing Industry*, c. 1910s, printed later. Checklist #87

Many newly arrived immigrant groups enter the labor market at the bottom. They provide some labor that other people will not do, at wages no-one else will accept. In the early years of this century, immigrant workers—largely in the garment industry—were active in the labor movement against sweatshop conditions and child labor. These workers, holding signs in Yiddish, English, Italian, and Russian march in a labor parade in New York.

Kuhli Photo Studio, *Goldie Mabovitz Meyerson—later famous as Golda Meir, Prime Minister of Israel—plays "Liberty" in American Pageant, Milwaukee, Wisconsin, May 18, 1919.* Checklist #101

As a young girl in 1906, Goldie Mabovitz departed with her family from Pinsk, Russia, and settled in Milwaukee. In this extraordinary photograph, teenager Mabovitz portrays the Statue of Liberty in a pageant. Standing next to "Abraham Lincoln," they welcome a group of Russian immigrants to the U.S. Goldie Mabovitz eventually became Golda Meir and served as the Prime Minister of Israel.

Unknown artist, *Norwegian Celebration at Humboldt Park, Chicago,* 1929. Checklist #106

Wrapping themselves in the flag, these buoyant young women illustrate the meaning of the old cliché. Their patriotism is undeniable. Overt displays of patriotism are more common among new immigrants than among succeeding generations.

Unknown artist, *Americanization class conducted by Board of Education*, c. 1900. Checklist #69

In this class, students of several different national origins studied not only the English language, but also U.S. Government structures and American customs and values.

Unknown artist, Untitled (women taking children for stroll), c. 1910. Checklist #90

Many diseases were related to overcrowded, unsanitary tenement living. Such dwellings suffered from poor ventilation. In the early years of this century, insistence on the benefits of fresh air reached fanatic proportions, with visiting nurses hammering open non-functional windows. This armada of mothers was organized by the Infant Welfare Society to go on regular walks, in all but the worst weather, to provide fresh air for tenement babies.

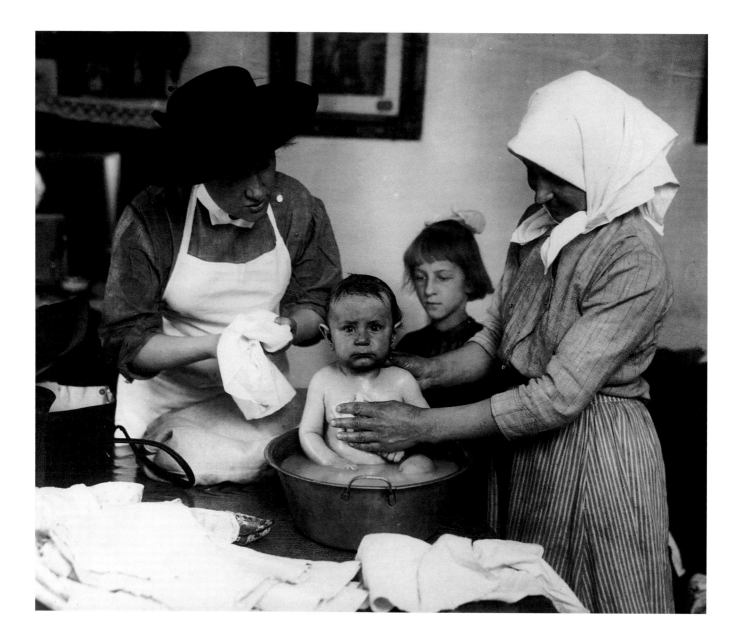

Unknown artist, Untitled (bathing child), c. 1915. Checklist #91

The Visiting Nurses Association covered all facets of childcare in their efforts to educate immigrant mothers in the skills of childrearing. This youngster provides his own editorial.

War brides have been a numerically small but important sector among immigrants to the U.S. While they may have been introduced to their spouses because of war, they helped to solidify the peace. It has been suggested that they be renamed "Brides of Peace."

American laws not only determined who could come to the United States, but also who could become citizens. Decades before Asian immigration had even begun, this country had already defined—by law—the complexion of U.S. citizens. The Naturalization Law of 1790 had specified that naturalized citizenship was to be reserved for "whites." This law remained in effect until 1952.

L. E. Edgeworth, *Chung Puu and Hawaiian Wife and Family*, 1920. Checklist #104

Hawaii was the principal point of entry for Asians, and many have settled there. Because the Chinese, Japanese, and Southeast Asian populations are so integral to the economic and social life of the Islands, racism toward these groups has been less virulent there than on the mainland. This Chinese gentleman and his Hawaiian wife identify a wealthy and integrated immigrant class. The boys hold books to symbolize their respect for education, and identify themselves as Hawaiian by their flower leis.

Unknown artist, *Japanese Boiler Tenders - left to right: Tokutaro Ishimi, Mr. Yamashiro and Mr. Karasaki, "Hoea" Sugar Mill, Kohala*, c. 1910. Checklist #96

Sugar was the foundation of the Hawaiian economy. The industry's labor needs were the primary lure for Japanese and Chinese workers. In the heat and humidity of Hawaii, these men fed the boiler furnaces.

Arthur Rothstein, *Mexican rehabilitation clients, Dona Ana County, New Mexico*, 1936, printed later. Checklist #112

After every harvest season, and certainly during the Great Depression, farm workers in the Southwest required government assistance to get through the year.

Arthur Rothstein, one of the great photographers of the Farm Security Administration, made important images of rural poverty in the dust bowl and along the great western migration routes. This is, perhaps, something of a 1936 Mexican American version of the famous painting, American Gothic by Grant Wood.

Dorothea Lange, *Braceros*, c. 1938 © The Dorothea Lange Collection, The Oakland Museum. Checklist #114

Prior to the official government Braceros program (initiated August, 1942), trainloads of Mexican workers were recruited and transported to southwestern states. In this way, millions promoted the dream and expectation of a better life in El Norte. At the same time, U.S. employers became addicted to cheap labor, free of union demands. It is jobs, not education or health care, that lure Mexican and Central American workers to the U.S.

The great documentary photographer Dorothea Lange powerfully illustrates a worker in 1938, when the tradition of transporting labor from Mexico to U.S. jobs was yet to be fully sanctioned by the Braceros agreement.

Russell Lee, *Mexican-American group at fiesta, Taos, New Mexico*, 1940, printed later. Checklist #117

Russell Lee's photographs often exhibit a deeply humane emotionalism. Here, an agricultural worker tries to cheer up his daughter at a fiesta. Festivals and religious ceremonies offer a concise window on the values and identity of a community. Photographers gravitate toward them for the drama of the pageantry as well as for the depth of information they provide about the participants.

Unknown artist, Untitled (Fannie Lui, Effie Lui, and Elizabeth Ng, Grace Faith Church, New York City), c. 1937. Checklist #113

These U.S.-born children of Chinese parents recite the Pledge of Allegiance while wearing the traditional garb of their progenitors.

Alexander Alland, *Home of Gypsies on Hester Street, New York City*, 1940. © 1995 Estate of Alexander Alland. Checklist #116

From a Jewish family living in Soviet-controlled Sebastopol, Alexander Alland fled to Constantinople in 1920, where he became an assistant to a Russian emigré photographer. He came to New York via Ellis Island on July 4, 1923. He provided the photographs for Portrait of New York, *a book published at the time of the 1939 New York World's Fair. Throughout the 1940s, Alland photographed among the many ethnic groups in and around New York City. His book of photographs and brief reminiscences,* American Counterpoint, *was published in 1943. In 1949 he was "blacklisted" for his association with leftist organizations, and he gave up making new photographs. Later in life, Alland authored two books of photographic history:* Jacob A. Riis: Photographer & Citizen *(1974) and* Jesse Tarbox Bels, First Woman News Photographer *(1978). A retrospective exhibition,* The Committed Eye: Alexander Alland's Photography, *was held at the Museum of the City of New York in 1991.*

These children and their parents inhabit the same Lower East Side of Manhattan tenements that have housed virtually every major wave of immigrants to New York. Today, the families on these steps are likely to be Vietnamese, Indian, or eastern European, among many other recent arrivals.

Hugo Summerville, *The C. Campa Labor Agency and W. J. Lewis of the Alamo City Employment Agency, distributing bread three times a day to Mexicans who are in distress, waiting to be sent to a job, March 22, 1924,* printed later. Checklist #107

World War I not only cut the flow of European immigrants, it also created labor shortages at the same time that industrial expansion came to the Southwest. These events led to enormous pressure for cheap labor. Large numbers of Mexican laborers were induced to work in the U.S. through industrial and agricultural lobbying, and were exempted from quota limits.

When the economy again turned sour, the vulnerable Mexican workers were shipped back home. In this photograph, the sign identifies the "Office to Hire Mexican Workers for all parts of the United States." The term Braceros is used here informally (Braceros literally means "arms" or "workers" as in the English term "hired hands"). In August, 1942, an official WWII United States agreement with Mexico provided temporary workers for the U.S., who would return to Mexico after a specified period. The official Braceros program lasted twenty-two years and brought millions of Mexican workers to the U.S.

NT AGENCY
S MEXICANOS.
UNIDOS.   Cr. 8622. Tr. 3854.

CITY EMPLOYMENT AGENCY
W.J. LEWIS Mgr.
854   PARA LAREDO EAGLE PASS

CASA DE CAMBIO MONTERREY
COMPRO VENDO DINERO
MEXICANO.

MONTERREY MONEY EXCHANGE
VENDEMOS GIROS PARA MEXICO
TODAS PARTES DE LA REPUBLICA MEXICANA

LA SULTANA MONTE
BARBER SHOP

SUMMERVILE
PHOTO

C. CAMPA #1 & W.J. LEWIS #2
1401 W. COMMERCE. ST   111. N. FRIO ST
SAN ANTONIO, TEXAS, MARCH 22-1924

ES A DAY TO MEXICANS WHO ARE IN DISTRESS WAITING TO BE SENT TO A JOB.

Eugene Omar Goldbeck, *Immigration Border Patrol, Laredo, Texas, February 1926, M.M. Hanson, Inspector in charge,* printed later. Checklist #108

This is the first photograph of the newly-established Border Patrol, which was commissioned in 1924. Little effort was made to control the Mexican border until WWII made U.S./Mexico border security seem more necessary.

The photographer, Eugene Omar Goldbeck, was noted for his intriguing panoramic photographs of both sweeping landscapes and large assemblages of people from all over the world.

Unknown artist. *FBI going through the belongings of a Japanese American family*, 1942. printed later. Checklist #118

In this telling image, a highly polished FBI agent rifles the family albums of a dispirited Japanese American family. He is searching for incriminating, subversive material which would cast doubt on this family's loyalty to the United States. The sense of cultural dissonance and legal powerlessness felt by the family is clear.

Clem Albers, *A young evacuee of Japanese ancestry waits with the family baggage before leaving by bus for an assembly center, Los Angeles, April, 1942.* Checklist #119

This image poignantly sums up the absurdity of Japanese WWII relocation. More than 120,000 Americans of Japanese ancestry, two-thirds of whom were U.S. citizens, were imprisoned without trial in 1942. Many of these citizens were children, who could scarcely have qualified as "security risks." No case of espionage was ever proven against any Japanese American individual. It was common for the media to attack first-generation Japanese immigrants for their unwillingness to become citizens, even though they were denied the right to U.S. citizenship by law.

Except for 525 citizens, Japanese Americans in Hawaii were not placed in internment camps in the same way those on the mainland were imprisoned. In Hawaii, the Japanese Americans were central to the economy. In California, they were seen as competition to the agricultural interests of the dominant culture.

Van Tassell, *For the War Relocation Authority* (U.S. government photo of Yo Takemoto Abe at the Paradise Flag Company, Denver, Colorado), 1943. Checklist #121.

This American propaganda photograph presents a patriotic young woman as a Japanese American Betsy Ross. But there are mixed messages. Is she happily engaged in patriotic work or proving her loyalty to a doubting government? In fact, Ms. Abe, who resides in Las Vegas, volunteered for agricultural work and was released from internment. She "topped beets" before working for the flag manufacturer. She identifies her motives as highly patriotic, but allows that "it was better than camp life and a lot better than topping beets."

Ansel Adams, *Still Life, Yonemitsu Family Quarters, Manzanar Relocation Center, October 1943.* Checklist #120

Ansel Adams made this poignant image at the Manzanar Relocation Camp, in the eastern Sierra near Lone Pine, California. It subtly identifies the powerful contradictions experienced by the imprisoned Yonemitsu family—son Robert, serving in the U.S. Army; a letter sent by him to his sister, whose rights he is unable to protect; a Christian image, indicating the adoption of American religious traditions that, regardless, are unable to unlock the prison gates and procure their freedom. All are understated elements in Adams's eloquent composition, quietly critical of the U.S. policy of Japanese American WWII internment.

Burt Glinn, *Swearing-in of New Citizens on Battleship* Missouri, *Seattle, Washington,* 1954. © 1995 Burt Glinn. Checklist #128

A group of new citizens recite the Pledge of Allegiance at their naturalization ceremony aboard the Missouri in Seattle, Washington. Numerous active-duty military personnel are also becoming citizens. A Japanese American couple in the front row stand on the very deck where nine years earlier, the Japanese government surrendered to allied forces at the end of WWII.

Burt Glinn, *Alien Registration, New York City*, c. 1950s. © 1995 Burt Glinn. Checklist #129

During and after WWII, the U.S. government required the registration of "enemy aliens"—those non-citizen residents from countries hostile to America. This family was expected to report their address, occupation, and whereabouts several times a year.

These Haitian refugees in 1980 foretold the masses of arrivals to come from Haiti in 1994 aboard similarly overcrowded vessels. It is hard to imagine three days at sea in such conditions.

Unknown artist, *Cuban refugees with varied expressions look at American coast off Key West. Coast Guard cutter* Diligence *in background*, c. 1980. Checklist #135

The Mariel Boatlift from Cuba in 1980 brought thousands of disaffected Cubans to the U.S., including some jail inmates and mentally-unstable individuals whom Castro wished to exile. The hope and anticipation on these faces is a common denominator of most American immigrants.

Charles Trainor, *Airlift list of Cuban refugees*, 1970. © 1995, Historical Museum of Southern Florida. Checklist #131

This photograph portrays anxious immigrants trying to find loved ones listed on arrival charts coordinated by Miami Cuban immigration agencies.

Alex Webb, *Christmas pageant, Cuban Social Club, Miami*, 1988. © 1995 Alex Webb/Magnum Photos. Checklist #154

Alex Webb is one of the nation's best known contemporary documentary photographers. While he has worked in many parts of the world, he has specialized in Florida, the Caribbean, and the U.S./Mexico border. He is known for his incisive use of color and silhouetted foreground figures.

Cuban immigrants from the early years of Castro's regime have, for the most part, done exceptionally well in southern Florida, and they have kept a very close eye on the fate of Cuba.

Alex Webb. *Cubans Training, Everglades,* 1988. © 1995 Alex Webb/Magnum Photos. Checklist #155

The majority of Cuban Americans living in the United States have longed for the day when the Castro regime will fall. Cuban immigrants train in the Everglades to hasten the demise of Cuban communism. A variety of military actions have been contemplated, from which the U.S. government has generally sought to distance itself.

Gary Monroe, *I.N.S. Krome Detention Center, Miami,* 1981. © 1995 Gary Monroe. Checklist #160

Krome is the largest detention center for new arrivals in the U.S. Thousands of applicants for refugee status await hearings and try to avoid boredom there. Haitians have had a hard time entering the U.S., as their government is non-communist and therefore not antagonistic to our own. In 1994, the U.S. occupied Haiti in order to reinstall and stabilize the elected government, and to stem the flow of emigrés traveling in homemade boats trying to reach Florida.

Gary Monroe, *Men's Building #8, I.N.S. Krome Detention Center, Miami,* 1981. © 1995 Gary Monroe. Checklist #161

Unrest at Krome Detention Center is continually monitored. As in other centers, such as facilities in Guantanamo where many Cuban rafters have been sequestered, residents at Krome feel imprisoned without trial. Their incarceration, in light of their search for greater freedom and opportunity, offers grim irony.

Mel Rosenthal, *Two Cambodian businessmen with a Buddhist monk at a celebration at the Church Avenue Refugee Center, Brooklyn, New York*, c. 1985. © 1995 Mel Rosenthal. Checklist #138

Cambodians ran for their lives in the mid-1970s when Pol Pot came to power. Mass relocation and genocide were carried out against all educated Cambodians, or anyone with contacts with the West. Approximately one-third of the country's entire population died of starvation, disease, or execution. In 1979, the Vietnamese invaded and deposed Pol Pot, and hundreds of thousands of people fled the country. More than 100,000 settled in the U.S. Some were rural villagers who had never even heard of the U.S. before they became refugees here.

The men in this photograph have made great efforts to adapt to their new reality. Here, they celebrate the Tet New Year.

Donna DeCesare, *Los Angeles Pico Union*, 1993. © 1993 Donna DeCesare. Checklist #152

The fifteen-year-old debutante festivities of Central America—the Quincianera —have successfully been transferred to the United States, and are an important element in the community life of Central American and Mexican immigrants.

These children are practicing their entrance to the ceremonies celebrating their older siblings.

Yale Strom, *Young girl from Bangladesh, Lower East Side, New York City*, 1995. © 1995 Yale Strom. Checklist #195

This teenager finds herself in a home decorated with words and slogans unreadable to her. U.S. urban street culture causes immigrants to be highly protective of their families and homes. The fortress character of the urban architecture illustrates one response to the problems of life in the "mean streets." Immigrants often inhabit sections of cities abandoned by previous arrivals, and thus vitalize sections that might otherwise be lost to the urban environment.

Facing page: **Audrey Gottlieb**, *Indian housewife paints 'rangoli' design at front entrance to her house, Queens, New York,* c. 1990. © 1995 Audrey Gottlieb. Checklist #146

An immigrant often surrounds herself with cultural manifestations that help her ease the transition to her new culture. This woman would have made these same designs at the entrance to her home in India. The drawings are traditionally made of dyed rice-flour, and are placed at the entrance of her home to welcome particular gods representing good fortune.

James Newberry, *Cambodian bride and groom at the conclusion of their day-and-half long wedding ceremony, which took place in a small apartment*, 1987. © 1995 James Newberry/Chicago Historical Society. Checklist #193

The ceremonies of birth, death, marriage, and coming-of-age central to most immigrant cultures last, in nearly pure form, for generations. They slowly take on elements from the dominant culture, but are often vestigially present ten or twelve generations after arrival.

Below: **Mel Rosenthal**, *Two women of the Hmong community, Syracuse, New York, May 1992.* © 1995 Mel Rosenthal. Checklist #140

The Vietnam War deeply impacted the Mein and Hmong tribesmen of Laos. Fleeing the Communist regimes, they dispersed around the western world; 70,000 ethnic Laotians, 10,000 Mein, and 60,000 Hmong arrived in the U.S.

These people have had great difficulty adjusting to life outside of their homelands. Their efforts to survive through severe disorientation is nothing short of heroic.

Facing page: **James Newberry**, *Grandfather and children at Japanese street festival. The children's father is of Japanese ancestry. Their mother is of European ancestry*, 1987. © 1995 James Newberry/Chicago Historical Society. Checklist #185

Older generations attempt to instill an understanding of the original culture in the younger ones, but in the end it is the children who generally teach the parents and grandparents how to be Americans. This reversal of roles is unsettling to many cultures, but for better or worse it is the most common form of cultural transmission in immigrant families.

Rick Rocomora, *Sergio Quinial, 68, with a picture of himself at age 21, hand-carried when he left the Philippines. "We can solve all our problems here in America except loneliness.",* 1993. © 1995 Rick Rocomora. Checklist #149

Many Filipinos joined the U.S. Armed Forces during WWII. They were promised full citizenship for their efforts; it took until 1992 for this promise to be fulfilled.

Facing page: **Pok Chi Lau**, *Nude beauty pictures in the bedroom of a Vietnamese Chinese newly wedded couple. The grandfather is eating in the kitchen, San Francisco,* 1981. © 1995 Pok Chi Lau. Checklist #133

Pok Chi Lau is an Associate Professor at the University of Kansas in the Department of Design, School of Fine Arts. He has exhibited his photographs extensively.

This photograph partially identifies the mixture of elements and influences inherent in a family adjusting to several divergent traditions.

Don Bartletti, *Pedestrian Barrier and Warning Sign*, 1993. © 1995 Don Bartletti, *Los Angeles Times*. Checklist #168

This ominous sign has become common around San Diego. It identifies families of undocumented arrivals who dash across highways to avoid apprehension. Fences are erected down the center of roads to prevent dangerous crossings.

For decades, U.S. agricultural and business interests have solicited and employed undocumented Latin Americans. As employment opportunities still abound in the U.S. alongside scant opportunity in Latin America, our government has little chance of completely eliminating illegal border crossings.

Don Bartletti, *Interstate Pedestrians*, 1989. © 1995 Don Bartletti, *Los Angeles Times*. Checklist #169

This form of border crossing has caused numerous deaths and frightens motorists, police and, of course, the pedestrians themselves. They, more than anyone else, understand the seriousness of their endeavor. Like many immigrants who brave difficult living and working conditions—a life of extreme limitation, the scorn of the populace, poor wages, and no security—they would not attempt to do this but for extraordinary initiative and exceptional needs.

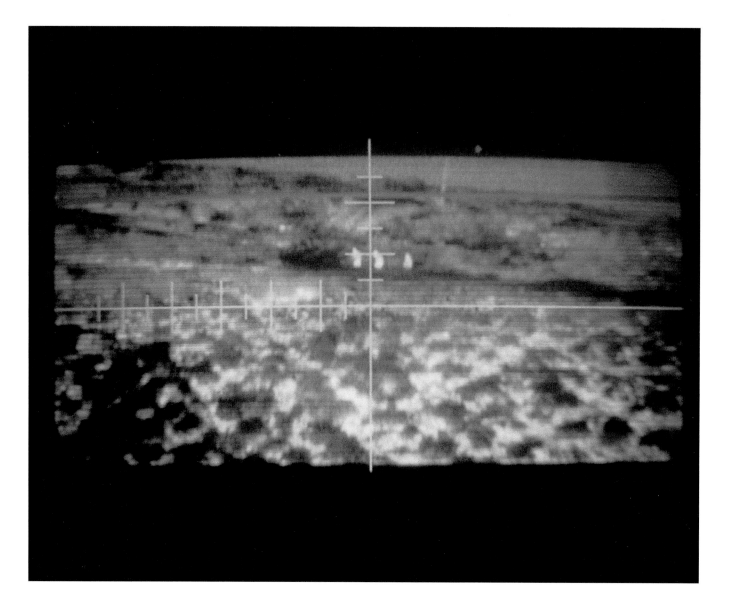

Dave Gatley, *Three ghostly figures emerge from behind a hill, as seen on the screen of an infra-red scope used to penetrate the almost total darkness near the border. Their movements will be radioed to the nearest Border Patrol unit*, 1992. © 1995 Dave Gatley. Checklist #166

The effort to control the flow of illegal immigration, particularly along the Mexican border, has intensified in recent years as the numbers of Mexican and Central American arrivals has escalated. New approaches by the Immigration and Naturalization Service include intense lighting, a triple fence system, and thousands of border agents. The number of undocumented crossings has been greatly reduced by these efforts.

Don Bartletti, *Border Opinions*, 1991. © 1995 Don Bartletti, *Los Angeles Times*. Checklist #171

Politicians and nativists have worked strenuously to block illegal immigration. In areas like San Diego, the impact of undocumented workers has been felt strongly, particularly by lower-income resident workers. The volume of immigrants, both legal and illegal, has risen steadily since 1965. However, "the rate of immigration relative to the nation's base population is far below historic levels . . . the average rate of legal immigration between 1981 and 1990 reached a post-Depression high of 3.1 per 1,000 U.S. residents. This rate is below that of every decade between 1830 and 1930, and is about the same as the long-term immigration rate since American independence. Moreover, the percentage of foreign born people in the U.S. population has fallen from 8.89 in 1940 to 6.8 today." America is not being overrun by immigrants. Some other countries may be.

Source: *Utne Reader*, May/June, 1994

Don Bartletti, *Highway Camp, Encinitas, California,* 1989. © Don Bartletti. Checklist #172

Don Bartletti's powerful image of Central American workers sleeping above the freeway illustrates the abysmal conditions endured by the people who provide us with cheap food, clothing, and various forms of manual labor. Bartletti's long-term devotion to this subject matter has given him uncommon access to the lives of these workers.

Don Bartletti, *Survival Class*, 1988. © 1995 Don Bartletti, *Los Angeles Times*. Checklist #170

Volunteer teachers translate simple phrases into correct, if heavily accented, English in an encampment in northern San Diego County. Photographer Don Bartletti has produced some of the most insightful images of complex and dramatic border issues.

Don Bartletti, *Lupe Villasenor and Son Victor*, 1991. © Don Bartletti. Checklist #173

Victor Villasenor is a well-known writer. His book Rain of Gold *traces the story of his mother (pictured here at his side) as she struggled to overcome poverty in California after immigrating from Lluvia de Oro, Mexico.*

Facing page: **James Newberry**, *A & H Factory for Alternators-Starters-Batteries—Mr. Ahmed Elhadary, born in Cairo, Egypt*, 1987. © James Newberry/Chicago Historical Society. Checklist #184

New arrivals to the United States tend to be the most entrepreneurial sector of our community. They establish large numbers of small companies, and create jobs for other immigrants and long time residents alike. Their initiative brought them here, and their motivation to succeed is great.

Yale Strom, *Young girl from Palestine (West Bank), Dearborn, Michigan.* © 1995 Yale Strom. Checklist #196

Dearborn, Michigan, with its strong base of automotive manufacturing, is the center of a large population of Arab immigrant families. Yale Strom is a well-known photographer and Klezmer musician. He recently produced and directed his first feature length documentary film, The Last Klezmer, Leopold Kozlowski, His Life and Music.

In late 1995, Simon and Schuster will publish Yale Strom's photographic book, Quilted Landscapes, Immigrant Youth in America.

Facing page: **James Newberry**, *Slaughter of goats on the feast of Abraham. Mr. Mohammad Mazhar Hussaini (l.), Executive Director of the Islamic Food and Nutrition Council of America and Director of Halal Slaughter Certification Committee, supervising the Halal slaughter,* 1987. © 1995 James Newberry/Chicago Historical Society. Checklist #189

Photographer James Newberry has identified and accessed important communities of immigrants within the greater Chicago area, and has beautifully portrayed individuals representing those communities.

Eric Chu, *Paradise (vacationers from Westchester County, New York, sit next to their inner tubes while watching as a Cuban raft is cleared off the beach in affluent Boca Raton, Florida, August 24, 1994).* © 1994, Eric Chu/*The News* (Boca Raton, Florida). Checklist #201

Nowhere is current immigration pressure seen as ironically as in the affluent coastal regions of Florida. Cuban rafters, who successfully navigate through rough seas and shark-filled waters on the most unpromising crafts, land on the very beaches sought out by migrating New Yorkers for recreation. Unsightly reminders of poverty and desperation are quickly removed from view.

Audrey Gottlieb, *Bagpipers bleat Irish Americans to Prayer at St. Sebastian's Church, Woodside, Queens, New York*, c. 1990. © 1995 Audrey Gottlieb. Checklist #148

Bagpipes are most often associated with Scotland, but there is also an Irish tradition of bagpiping.

Nineteenth century Irish immigrants developed political power quickly. As Caucasians they were eligible for citizenship and suffrage. They arrived speaking English, which gave them a great advantage; their rate of becoming citizens was the highest of all immigrant groups. They came to stay. While an estimated 40–60 percent of Italian arrivals returned to Italy after a time, only 10 percent of the Irish returned to their homeland. By 1890, the Irish controlled most of the Democratic party organizations in northern cities.

Chester Higgins, Jr., *Asante King from Ghana, Diaspora King Seated in Court*, 1988. © 1995 Chester Higgins, Jr. Checklist #180

Chester Higgins, Jr. is a staff photographer for The New York Times. *Since the late 1960s he has photographed dignified manifestations of African American life for* Ebony, Life, Time, Fortune, Black Enterprise, *and many other publications. His large project on the life within communities of African descent includes a sub-theme on the multiplicity of religious observances. Here, a ceremony of the Akan-speaking people of Ghana is held in New York.*

Facing page: **Chester Higgins, Jr.**, *Brazilian Immigrant worships Oshun, African deity of fresh water and love*, 1989. © 1995 Chester Higgins, Jr. Checklist #181

The passage and transformation of African religions to the United States often found stop-over points in South America and the Caribbean Islands, where the rites and languages of worship were altered. The practices mixed with local customs and blended with Christian symbolism, as slaves were not permitted religious interests of their own. Today, these religions have strongly taken root and grown dramatically, often far beyond the African American or immigrant communities.

Chester Higgins, Jr., *Memorial to African ancestors who perished in Atlantic Ocean during transfer from Africa to American enslavement*, 1990. © 1995 Chester Higgins, Jr. Checklist #179

The social movements to raise African American consciousness in the 1960s, 1970s, and 1980s, has introduced numerous religious denominations, rituals, and cultural observances new to the United States. Here, an annual memorial service is enacted honoring the approximately one million African slaves who died en route to the western hemisphere.

Audrey Gottlieb, *Brahmin priest chants and lays clay Ganesha elephant God into muddy bed of Flushing Meadow Lake, Queens, New York*, c. 1990. © 1995 Audrey Gottlieb. Checklist #144

Religions perform major preservative functions, ensuring continuities of belief, rites, the familiar language of chants, prayers and stories, the trusted sameness of things—priestly garments, icons, and other aids to worship. Photographs of priests and rituals identify both strangeness and spirituality, reminding wary viewers that the new immigrants are God-fearing people, at least in their own way.

James Newberry, *Msgr. John Naffah, pastor and founder of Our Lady of Lebanon Maronite Catholic Church of Chicago, (425 N. Hillside Ave. Hillside, IL), born in Jounieh, Lebanon,* 1987. © 1995 James Newberry/Chicago Historical Society. Checklist #191

Lebanese Christian communities have long immigrated to the United States. Their Moslem countrymen have come only since the mid-1960s, with larger numbers arriving during the Lebanese Civil War in the 1980s.

James Newberry, *Monks of Thai Buddhist Temple*, 1987. © James Newberry/Chicago Historical Society. Checklist #187

Religious teachers and holy men of many religions arrive from their native countries to minister to the spiritual needs of their dispersed flocks. Our nation was created by religious outcasts, and spiritual freedom was highest on their list of freedoms for the new country. While some seek to identify American religious interests in a very narrow way, the Constitution is clear on these freedoms and their most expansive interpretation.

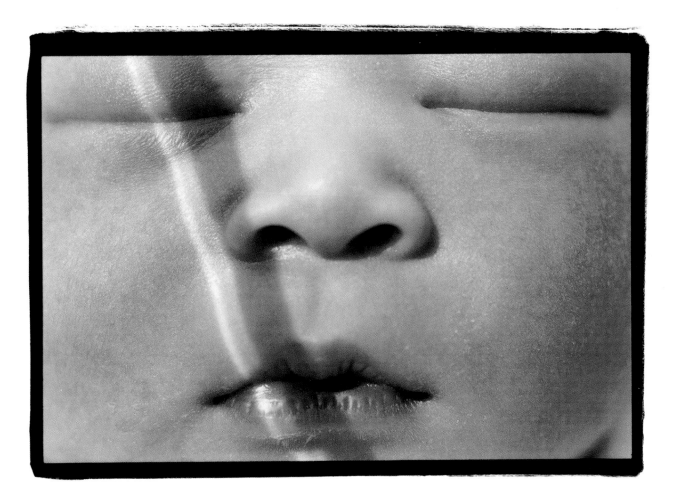

Pok Chi Lau. *Tyler Kakeru Lau, son of the photographer, first day as an Asian American, Lawrence, Kansas,* 1988.
© 1995 Pok Chi Lau. Checklist #134

The photographer identifies his son as Asian American, a designation that is both general and specific. It identifies a sub-group of Americans, but does not identify a particular ethnicity from among the many Asian nations. In fact, Tyler Kakeru Lau's face is American.

1562 A group of French Huguenots establishes a colony on Parris Island, near Beaufort, South Carolina, but abandons it after two years.

1565 The first permanent Spanish settlement in the United States is established in St. Augustine, Florida.

1607 The first permanent English settlement is founded at Jamestown, Virginia.

1614 The first major Dutch settlement is founded near Albany, New York.

1619 The first shipload of twenty indentured African slaves arrives at Jamestown.

1620 The Pilgrims arrive in America and establish a colony at Plymouth, Massachusetts.

1629 Five shiploads of Puritans, totaling about 900 people, arrive in Massachusetts Bay.

1634 Lord Baltimore establishes Maryland as a refuge for English Catholics.

1654 The first Jewish immigrants to the New World (originating from Brazil) settle in New Amsterdam.

1683 Mennonites, the first German settlers to reach the New World, arrive in Pennsylvania.

1685 A small group of Huguenots settles in South Carolina.

1697 The business of slavery expands rapidly as New Englanders find it extremely profitable.

1707 Scottish migration to the New World begins; many Scots become indentured servants in tobacco colonies in New York.

1717 An Act of Parliament in England legalizes transportation of criminals to the American colonies as punishment; contractors begin regular shipments of prisoners from British jails to Virginia and Maryland.

1718 Large-scale Scottish and Irish immigration begins, with most settling first in New England, then in Maryland and Pennsylvania.

1740 British Parliament enacts the Naturalization Act, conferring British citizenship on colonial immigrants in the hope of encouraging Jewish emigration. Jews enjoy a greater degree of political and religious freedom in the American colonies than anywhere in the world at this time.

1755 French Acadians are expelled from Nova Scotia on suspicion of disloyalty; they settle in Louisiana.

1771-73 A depression in the Irish Ulster linen trade and an acute

agrarian crisis bring a new influx of Scottish and Irish immigrants — approximately 10,000 annually — to the New World.

1776 The American Revolution begins.

1789 The French Revolution forces aristocrats and royalist sympathizers to emigrate to the newly established United States of America.

1791 Negro revolt in Santo Domingo forces 10,000-20,000 French exiles to seek refuge in the United States, principally in towns along the Atlantic seaboard.

1795 The U.S. Naturalization Act is passed, requiring a residence period of five years and a renunciation of foreign allegiances and titles of nobility as prerequisites for U.S. citizenship.

1803 The British Passenger Act limits the numbers of people to be carried by emigrant ships, effectively halting Irish emigration for many years.

1807 The U.S. Congress prohibits the importation of African slaves (already prohibited by some states, including Delaware in 1776; Virginia, 1778; Maryland, 1783; South Carolina, 1787; North Carolina, 1794; Georgia, 1798).

1810 By this date, the U.S. population is 7,239,881, including 1,211,364 slaves and 186,746 free Blacks.

1814 This year marks the beginning of the first great wave of European immigration: 5 million immigrants will arrive in the U.S. between 1815 and 1860.

1819 On March 2nd, an immigration law requiring a numerical tally of immigrants is passed. For the first time, statistics on the number of new arrivals will be kept by the government.

1825 The first group of Norwegian immigrants, in the sloop *Restaurationen*, arrive in the U.S. They leave behind overpopulated farms and a weakening economy.

1830 By this date, the U.S. population is 12,866,020. During the next decade more than 573,000 immigrants will arrive in the United States.

The Polish revolution takes place, and public land in Illinois is allotted by Congress to refugees from the revolution.

1837 During a time of great financial panic, "nativists" complain that immigration lowers wage levels, contributes to the decline of the apprenticeship system and generally depresses labor conditions.

Steerage passage for German immigrants leaving from the port of Bremen is $16.

1841 Five shipwrecked Japanese are rescued at sea by an American vessel. Four are put ashore at Honolulu, but the fifth, Manjuro Nakahama, sails on to the mainland to become America's first Japanese immigrant.

1845 A Nativist political party is founded, with minimal support in fourteen states. However, ten years later, a similar anti-immigrant "Know-Nothing" political party reaches its peak of support.

1846 Crop failures in Germany and Holland lead thousands of dispossessed to emigrate to the U.S.

1846-48 A *Phytophthora* infestation ravages the Irish potato fields resulting in mass starvation (more than 1 million people die) and emigration of 3 million survivors to the United States. The history of Ireland is forever altered as a result.

1848 The treaty of Guadalupe-Hidalgo ends the Mexican-American War. According to the terms of the treaty, the United States acquires Colorado, Arizona, New Mexico, Texas, California, and parts of Utah and Nevada, in exchange for $15 million.

1849 Discovery of gold in California lures people from all over the world, including many from China, to work mining claims.

1851 250,000 Irish and 20,000 French immigrants arrive in America.

1854 German immigrants account for more than 50 percent of the 400,000 new arrivals seeking refuge in America during this one year.

1855 Castle Garden, the first "immigrant depot," opens in New York City.

1860 New York becomes the "largest Irish city in the world," with 203,760 Irish born citizens

out of a total city-wide population of 805,651.

1862 The Homestead Act grants willing settlers title to 160 acres of farm land, provided that the acreage will be tilled for five years. By 1890, some 375,000 homesteaders receive 48 million acres of land, displacing thousands of native peoples.

1861-65 The American Civil War; immigrants serve on both sides of the conflict.

1863 President Lincoln signs the Emancipation Proclamation into law, freeing slaves in America.

1864 To meet the labor crisis caused by the Civil War, Congress passes legislation to encourage immigration.

1882 The first federal immigration law bars "lunatics, idiots, convicts and those likely to become public charges." The Chinese Exclusion Act denies entry to Chinese laborers for a period of ten years (this law will be renewed in 1892; Chinese immigration will be suspended indefinitely in 1902, and many immigrants will return home).

Violent anti-Semitism in Russia causes a sharp rise in Jewish emigration to the U.S.

1883 The Southern Immigration Association is formed to promote European immigration to the Southern United States. Without slaves to work the land there is a great need for cheap labor, which immigrants often provide.

1886 The statue of "Liberty Enlightening the World" is dedicated on

October 28th by President Grover Cleveland. At the base of the statue, a poem by immigrant Emma Lazarus proclaims America as a place of welcome for "tired, poor, huddled masses yearning to breathe free . . ."

At the same time the Statue of Liberty proclaims America's welcome to immigrants, "nativism" is once again a growing political movement in America seeking ways to keep the "foreigners" out.

1891 Congress adds health restrictions to immigration policies. Pogroms in Russia force another wave of Jewish emigration to theU.S.

1892 Ellis Island replaces Castle Garden in New York as a reception center for immigrants.

1894 The Immigration Restriction League is organized to spearhead an immigration-restrictionist movement for the next twenty-five years. The movement emphasizes a distinction between "old" immigrants (northern and western Europeans) and "new" (southern and eastern Europeans).

1898 Hawaii is annexed by the U.S. as a territory. Nearly 60,000 Japanese residing in Hawaii at the time proceed to the mainland without passport restrictions.

1905 The Japanese and Korean Exclusion League is formed by organized labor to protest the influx of "coolie" labor, and a perceived threat to the living standards of American workers.

1907-08 A "gentleman's agreement" between the Japanese and U.S. governments denies passports to Japanese laborers emigrating from Japan; however, the agreement fails to satisfy West Coast exclusionists.

1910 The Mexican Revolution sends thousands of peasants to the U.S. border seeking safety and employment.

1913 The California state legislature passes an Alien Land Law, effectively barring Japanese, Koreans and Chinese, as "aliens ineligible for citizenship," from owning agricultural land in the state.

1914-18 World War I ends the first great wave of mass European migration to the U.S.

1916 Madison Grant's *The Passing of the Great Race* calls for the exclusion of "inferior" Alpine, Mediterranean, and Jewish "breeds" based on racist attitudes toward these immigrants.

1921 The Emergency Immigration Restriction Law introduces a quota system, heavily weighted in favor of northern and western Europeans, all but slamming the door on southern and eastern Europeans. An immediate slump in immigration results.

1923 The Ku Klux Klan, at heart a virulently anti-immigrant movement, reaches its peak strength.

1929 The National Origins Act becomes operative. The Stock market crashes and the Great Depression begins. Political movements demand that immigration be further reduced during this economic crisis.

1933 Hitler becomes Germany's chancellor and he implements a sweeping anti-Semitic campaign. Jewish refugees from Nazi Germany flee to the U.S., despite the quota system.

1934 The Tydings-McDuffie Act limits Filipino immigration to the United States to fifty persons per year.

1939 World War II begins in Europe.

1941 U.S. enters WWII in December. Thousands of immigrants join the armed forces and support the allied effort.

1942 The U.S. government forcibly evacuates Americans of Japanese descent from the Pacific Coast to detention camps. They become victims of deep-seated suspicion, animosity, and the frequently-unjustified fear of espionage and sabotage.

The *Bracero* program strongly encourages Mexicans to come to America as farm and agricultural workers, due to the labor shortage created by WWII. The program is finally terminated in 1964.

1945 Large-scale Puerto Rican immigration begins as people try to escape crushing poverty on the island, only to find similar conditions in New York.

1948 The Displaced Persons Act, signed by President Truman, opens America to 205,000 Europeans displaced by the ravages of WWII.

1952 The McCarran-Walter Immigration and Naturalization Act is passed, extending token immigration quotas to Asian nations, as thanks for their support of the Allies in WWII.

1954   Ellis Island closes as a point of entry for immigrants. It is later refurbished and reopens as a national museum and historic landmark.

1957   Special legislation passes Congress to admit Hungarian refugees, following the Soviet crackdown on Hungary's bid for independence.

1960   Cuban refugees flee to the U.S. as Fidel Castro leads a communist revolution.

1963   Congress, urged by President Kennedy, passes new legislation eliminating the National Origins quota system.

1965   The Cuban Refugee Airlift begins, six years after Fidel Castro assumes power in Cuba. For the next eight years, Cubans are admitted to the U.S. under special quotas. The Immigration Act, signed by President Johnson, eliminates race, creed, and nationality as a basis for admission to the United States. As soon as the old quota system is removed, immigration from non-European nations increases sharply.

1970   President Nixon amends the 1965 Immigration Act, further liberalizing U.S. immigration policy.

1979   Congress appropriates more than $334 million in rescue and resettlement funds for Vietnamese "boat people."

China, the most populous country on Earth, institutes an aggressive policy aimed at limiting the number of children to one-per-family. This policy results in hundreds of Chinese people emigrating to the United States, where no such government policy exists.

1980   A new wave of Cuban refugees embark for the U.S. on the "Freedom Flotilla."

1986   Congress passes the Immigration Reform and Control Act, which, for the first time, makes it illegal for employers to hire illegal aliens.

1991   Legal immigration to the United States nears 2 million people, up from 600,000 the previous year. By 1992, immigrants add another one million people to the population.

1993   As the number of illegal aliens in the U.S. reaches an estimated 3 million, pressure mounts in Southern California and elsewhere to curb immigration.

1994   The decline of the Cuban economy, due to the U.S. economic blockade and the dissolution of the Soviet Union, leads thousands of Cubans to board makeshift rafts and embark on a life-threatening journey toward Florida. Most are picked up by the U.S. Coast Guard and held in detention facilities for immigration hearings. A few are allowed in as refugees.

Political repression in Haiti swells the number of refugees. The U.S. prepares to go to war to restore a functioning, democratically-elected government, and thereby stop emigration; U.S. troops occupy Haiti for more than six months.

California voters support state Proposition 187, to limit state benefits for health care and education for undocumented immigrants. Other states begin drafting similar policies. Lawsuits on behalf of undocumented immigrants are filed in California on constitutional grounds and decisions are pending.

1995   Chinese organized crime, working from a base in Central America, continues to orchestrate large-scale, undocumented migration of Chinese people to the U.S., for huge financial gain.

With political pressure against immigrants once more on the rise, federal politicians try to repeal constitutional ammendments granting citizenship to anyone born in the United States, regardless of the legal status of parents. Many long-time "resident aliens" apply for U.S. citizenship. ◀

BY CATHERINE S. HERLIHY

A Nation of Strangers

Reframing America

Tracing Cultures

The Museum of Photographic Arts, the Center for Creative Photography, and The Friends of Photography have created three separate, but intertwined, photographic exhibitions. In response, I have assembled a bibliography of contemporary scholarly and juvenile titles that may help answer questions posed by the exhibition images.

A Nation of Strangers was curated by Arthur Ollman and Vicki Goldberg at the Museum of Photographic Arts. This title suggests that we must make an effort to learn about each other. We came from different places; we came at different times; we faced different welcomes.

Under the heading, "Groups of People," there are six categories based on continents. Are there patterns to see in the timing of immigration? If there are immigration surges, were they triggered by war or economic woes? Are many African Americans the only people whose ancestors came because of brute force? Do groups of people who feel threatened by immigrants who are not like themselves identify with American Indians? I included two categories that are not geographical. I let my empathy for women immigrants show in one section. Perhaps other people will have an interest in Jewish people; I included one title about Moroccan Jews in the 'Americans who are also Jewish' section.

Reframing America was curated by Terence Pitts at the Center for Creative Photography. This show illustrates the aesthetic ideas refugees from Hitler brought to the United States. Those ideas stimulated new questions and work throughout the nation. I included some titles to discuss the influence of their ideas.

Tracing Cultures was curated by Andy Grundberg at The Friends of Photography. How are people of different cultures treated when they immigrate to the United States? To help answer that question, I included examples from newspaper coverage in the 1880s and in the 1980s as well as titles on the portrayal of immigrants in movies and television. Have different groups of people been judged on factors outside of their control? Did your ancestors arrive during the deep depression in the eastern states during the 1890s? Or did your ancestors arrive at that same time on the west coast where their labor was desperately needed? Do you think that Catholic Italians had a harder time than the Catholic Irish since Italian immigrants had to learn a new language?

The Museum of Photographic Arts, the Center for Creative Photography, and The Friends of Photography each support educational outreach programs. To reflect this effort, I have included a selection of juvenile non-fiction and fiction. There are also a few titles that parents, librarians, and teachers might use to stimulate discussions on immigration and assimilation.

I hope you will find in my bibliography several titles that pique your interest. The amount of recent work on immigrants is staggering and I have had to be selective because of space constraints. I limited myself to titles published since 1983. I am very conscious of our decision to include English language books only. Remember, too, that my choices are from titles written and published. I can only point you to an ocean of recently published material.

Historians regularly re-examine earlier work in light of new information and questions. Photographers formulate styles to mark their perspectives. My bibliography is also a 'point of entry' into the ideas of immigration and racism, assimilation and multi-culturalism.

Thanks to Kevin Walden for his technical assistance. ◄

IMMIGRATION

HISTORY

Barringer, Herbert R., Robert W. Gardner, and Michael J. Levin. *Asians and Pacific Islanders in the United States.* New York: Russell Sage Foundation, 1993.

Brown, Wesley, and Amy Ling, eds. *Visions of America: Personal Narratives from the Promised Land.* New York: Persea Books, 1993.

Cooke, Alistair. *America. The Huddled Masses.* [videorecording] New York: Ambrose Video Publishers, 1988.

Daniels, Roger. *Coming to America: A History of Immigration and Ethnicity in American Life.* New York: Harper Collins, 1990.

Dublin, Thomas, ed. *Immigrant Voices: New Lives in America, 1773-1986.* Urbana, Ill.: University of Illinois Press, 1993.

Glazer, Nathan, ed. *Clamor at the Gates: The New American Immigration.* San Francisco, Calif.: Institute of Contemporary Studies Press, 1985.

Jacobson, Matthew Frye. *Special Sorrows: The Diasporic Imagination of Irish, Polish, and Jewish Immigrants in the United States.* Cambridge, Mass.: Harvard University Press, 1995.

Jones, Maldwyn Allen. *American Immigration.* Chicago, Ill.: University of Chicago Press, 1992.

Kilian, Pamela. *Ellis Island: Gateway to the American Dream.* New York: Crescent Books, 1991.

Mendoza, Alejandro G. *The United States Immigration History Timeline.* New York: Terra Firma Press, 1990.

Morrison, Joan, and Charlotte Fox Zabusky, comps. *American Mosaic: The Immigrant Experience in the Words of Those Who Lived It.* Pittsburgh, Penn.: University of Pittsburgh Press, 1993.

Muller, Thomas. *Immigrants and the American City.* New York: New York University Press, 1993.

Namias, June, comp. *First Generation: In the Words of Twentieth-Century American Immigrants.* Urbana, Ill.: University of Illinois Press, 1992.

Perlmann, Joel. *Ethnic Differences: Schooling and Social Structure Among the Irish, Italians, Jews, and Blacks in an American City, 1880-1935.* New York: Cambridge University Press, 1988.

Portes, Alejandro, and Rubén G. Rumbaut. *Immigrant America: A Portrait.* Berkeley, Calif.: University of California Press, 1990.

Reimers, David M. *Still the Golden Door: The Third World Comes to America.* New York: Columbia University Press, 1992.

Stolarik, M. Mark, ed. *Forgotten Doors: The Other Ports of Entry to the United States.* Philadelphia, Penn.: Balch Institute Press, 1988.

Ueda, Reed. *Postwar Immigrant America: a Social History.* Boston, Mass.: St. Martin's Press, 1994.

Watkins, Susan Cotts, ed. *After Ellis Island: Newcomers and Natives in the 1910 Census.* New York: Russell Sage Foundation, 1994.

Yans-McLaughlin, Virginia, ed. *Immigration Reconsidered: History, Sociology, and Politics.* New York: Oxford University Press, 1990.

GOVERNMENT POLICY

Barbour, William, ed. *Illegal Immigration.* San Diego, Calif.: Greenhaven Press, 1994.

Bean, Frank D., Georges Vernez, and Charles B. Keely. *Opening and Closing the Doors: Evaluating Immigration Reform and Control.* Santa Monica, Calif.: Rand Corp., 1989.

Bean, Frank D., Jurgen Schmandt, and Sidney Weintraub, eds. *Mexican and Central American Population and U.S. Immigration Policy.* Austin, Tex.: University of Texas Press, 1989.

Briggs, Vernon M. *Mass Immigration and the National Interest.* Armonk, N.Y.: M.E. Sharpe, 1992.

Calavita, Kitty. *Inside the State: The Bracero Program, Immigration, and the I.N.S.* New York: Routledge, 1992.

Corcoran, Mary P. *Irish Illegals: Transients between Two Societies.* Westport, Conn.: Greenwood Press, 1993.

Hing, Bill Ong. *Making and Remaking Asian America Through Immigration Policy, 1850-1990.* Stanford, Calif.: Stanford University Press, 1993.

Immigration Law Enforcement Monitoring Project. *Sealing Our Borders: The Human Toll.* Philadelphia, Penn.: American Friends Service Committee, 1992.

Koehn, Peter H. *Refugees from Revolution: U.S. Policy and Third-World*

Migration. Boulder, Col.: Westview Press, 1991.

Komatsu, Sylvia. *The Other Side of the Border.* [videorecording] Washington, D.C.: PBS Video, 1987.

Kraut, Alan M. *Silent Travelers: Germs, Genes, and the "Immigrant Menace."* New York: Basic Books, 1994.

LeMay, Michael C. *From Open Door to Dutch Door: an Analysis of U.S. Immigration Policy Since 1820.* New York: Praeger, 1987.

Loescher, Gil, and John A. Scanlan. *Calculated Kindness: Refugees and America's Half-Open Door, 1945 to the Present.* New York: Free Press, 1986.

Mills, Nicolaus, ed. *Arguing Immigration: The Debate Over the Changing Face of America.* New York: Simon & Schuster, 1994.

Mitchell, Christopher, ed. *Western Hemisphere Immigration and United States Foreign Policy.* University Park, Penn.: Pennsylvania State University Press, 1992.

Polanco, Richard G., and Grace Napolitano. *Making Immigration Policy Work in the United States.* Sacramento, Calif.: California Latino Legislative Caucus, 1993.

Rolph, Elizabeth S. *Immigration Policies: Legacy from the 1980s and Issues for the 1990s.* Santa Monica, Calif.: Rand Corp., 1992.

Smith, Michael P., and Bernadette Tarallo. *California's Changing Faces: New Immigrant Survival Strategies and State Policy.* Berkeley, Calif.: California Policy Seminar, University of California Press, 1993.

Suro, Roberto. *Remembering the American Dream: Hispanic Immigration and National Policy.* New York: Twentieth Century Fund Press, 1994.

Teitelbaum, Michael S. *Latin Migration North: The Problem for U.S. Foreign Policy.* New York: Council on Foreign Relations, 1985.

Tucker, Robert W., Charles B. Keely, and Linda Wrigley, eds. *Immigration and U.S. Foreign Policy.* Boulder, Col.: Westview Press, 1990.

LABOR

Asis, Maruja Milagros B. *To the United States and into the Labor Force: Occupational Expectations of Filipino and Korean Immigrant Women.* Honolulu, Hawaii: East-West Center, 1991.

Bustamante, Jorge A., Clark W. Reynolds, and Raúl A. Hinojosa Ojeda, eds. *U.S.-Mexico Relations: Labor Market Interdependence.* Stanford, Calif. Stanford University Press, 1992.

Calavita, Kitty. *U.S. Immigration Law and the Control of Labor, 1820-1924.* Orlando, Fla.: Academic Press, 1984.

Cornelius, Wayne A., and Philip L. Martin. *The Uncertain Connection: Free Trade and Mexico-U.S. Migration.* San Diego, Calif.: Center for U.S.-Mexican Studies, UCSD, 1993.

Debouzy, Marianne, ed. *In the Shadow of the Statue of Liberty: Immigrants, Workers, and Citizens in the American Republic, 1880-1920.* Urbana, Ill.: University of Illinois Press, 1992.

Desbarats, Jacqueline. *Economic Consequences of Indochinese Chain Migration to California.* Berkeley, Calif.: California Policy Seminar, University of California Press, 1987.

Diaz-Briquets, Sergio, and Sidney Weintraub, eds. *Determinants of Emigration From Mexico, Central America, and the Caribbean.* Boulder, Col.: Westview Press, 1991.

Fix, Michael, ed. *The Paper Curtain: Employer Sanctions' Implementation, Impact, and Reform.* Santa Monica, Calif.: Rand Corp., 1991.

Guerin-Gonzales, Camille. *Mexican Workers and American Dreams: Immigration, Repatriation, and California Farm Labor, 1900-1939.* New Brunswick, N.J.: Rutgers University Press, 1994.

Heppel, Monica L., and Sandra L. Amendola. *Immigration Reform and Perishable Crop Agriculture: Compliance or Circumvention?* Lanham, Md.: University Press of America, 1992.

Holter, Darryl, ed. *Beyond the Free Trade Debate: Labor's Future in California and Mexico.* Los Angeles, Calif.: Center for Labor Research and Education, University of California, 1993.

Keil, Hartmut, and John B. Jentz, eds. *German Workers in Chicago: A Documentary History of Working-Class Culture from 1850 to World War I.* Urbana, Ill.: University of Illinois Press, 1988.

Knouse, Stephen B., Paul Rosenfeld, and Amy Culbertson, eds. *Hispanics in the Workplace.* Newbury Park, Calif.: Sage Publications, 1992.

Lamphere, Louise, Alex Stepick, and Guillermo Grenier, eds. *Newcomers in the Workplace: Immigrants and the*

Restructuring of the U.S. Economy. Philadelphia, Penn.: Temple University Press, 1994.

Martin, Philip L. *Trade and Migration: NAFTA and Agriculture.* Washington, D.C.: Institute for International Economics, 1993.

Monto, Alexander. *The Roots of Mexican Labor Migration.* Westport, Conn.: Praeger, 1994.

Ronfeldt, David F., and Monica Ortiz de Oppermann. *Mexican Immigration, U.S. Investment, and U.S.-Mexican Relations.* Santa Monica, Calif.: Rand Corp., 1990.

Smith, Robert. *Mexican Immigrant Women in New York City's Informal Economy.* New York: Columbia University-New York University Consortium, 1992.

Vernez, Georges, and Kevin McCarthy. *Meeting the Economy's Labor Needs Through Immigration: Rationale and Challenges.* Santa Monica, Calif.: Rand Corp., 1990.

Waldinger, Roger David. *Through the Eye of the Needle: Immigrants and Enterprise in New York's Garment Trades.* New York: New York University Press, 1986.

GROUPS OF PEOPLE

AMERICANS FROM AFRICA

Center for Afroamerican and African Studies (University of Michigan). *Black Immigration and Ethnicity in the United States: An Annotated Bibliography.* Westport, Conn.: Greenwood Press, 1985.

Gatewood, Willard B. *Aristocrats of Color: The Black Elite, 1880-1920.* Bloomington, Ind.: Indiana University Press, 1990.

Hopson, Darlene Powell, and Derek S. Hopson. *Different and Wonderful: Raising Black Children in a Race-Conscious Society.* New York: Simon & Schuster, 1992.

Jhally, Sut, and Justin Lewis. *Enlightened Racism: The Cosby Show, Audiences, and the Myth of the American Dream.* Boulder, Col.: Westview Press, 1992.

Jordan, June. *Technical Difficulties: African-American Notes on the State of the Union.* New York: Pantheon Books, 1992.

Mathabane, Mark. *Kaffir Boy in America: An Encounter with Apartheid.* New York: Scribner's, 1989.

Woldemikael, Tekle Mariam. *Becoming Black American: Haitians and American Institutions in Evanston, Illinois.* New York: AMS Press, 1989.

AMERICANS FROM ASIA

Barkan, Elliott Robert. *Asian and Pacific Islander Migration to the United States: A Model of New Global Patterns.* Westport, Conn.: Greenwood Press, 1992.

Chan, Sucheng, ed. *Entry Denied: Exclusion and the Chinese Community in America, 1882-1943.* Philadelphia, Penn.: Temple University Press, 1991.

Daniels, Roger. *Asian America: Chinese and Japanese in the United States Since 1850.* Seattle, Wash.: University of Washington Press, 1988.

Daniels, Roger. *Prisoners Without Trial: Japanese Americans in World War II.* New York: Hill and Wang, 1993.

Dasgupta, Sathi Sengupta. *On the Trail of an Uncertain Dream: Indian Immigrant Experience in America.* New York: AMS Press, 1989.

Gibson, Margaret A. *Accommodation Without Assimilation: Sikh Immigrants in an American High School.* Ithaca, N.Y.: Cornell University Press, 1988.

Ichioka, Yuji, ed. *Views From Within: The Japanese American Evacuation and Resettlement Study.* Los Angeles, Calif.: Asian American Studies Center, UCLA, 1989.

Kimura, Yukiko. *Issei: Japanese Immigrants in Hawaii.* Honolulu, Hawaii: University of Hawaii Press, 1988.

Patterson, Wayne. *The Korean Frontier in America: Immigration to Hawaii, 1896-1910.* Honolulu, Hawaii: University of Hawaii Press, 1988.

Reed, Dennis. *Japanese Photography in America, 1920-1940.* Los Angeles, Calif.: Japanese American Cultural & Community Center, 1985.

Takaki, Ronald T. *Ethnic Islands: The Emergence of Urban Chinese America.* New York: Chelsea House, 1994.

Tamura, Eileen. *Americanization, Acculturation, and Ethnic Identity: The Nisei Generation in Hawaii.* Urbana, Ill.: University of Illinois Press, 1994.

Taylor, Sandra C. *Jewel of the Desert: Japanese American Internment at Topaz.* Berkeley, Calif.: University of California Press, 1993.

Tenhula, John. *Voices From Southeast Asia: The Refugee Experience in the United States.* New York: Holmes & Meier, 1991.

Yamato, Alexander et al. *Asian Americans in the United States.* Dubuque, Iowa: Kendall/Hunt Pub. Co., 1993.

Americans from Europe

Anderson, Virginia DeJohn. *New England's Generation: The Great Migration and the Formation of Society and Culture in the Seventeenth Century.* New York: Cambridge University Press, 1991.

Erickson, Charlotte. *Leaving England: Essays on British Emigration in the Nineteenth Century.* Ithaca, N.Y.: Cornell University Press, 1994.

Ewart, Shirley. *Cornish Mining Families of Grass Valley, California.* New York: AMS Editorial Dept., 1989.

Hardwick, Susan Wiley. *Russian Refuge: Religion, Migration, and Settlement on the North American Pacific Rim.* Chicago, Ill.: University of Chicago Press, 1993.

Hoerder, Dirk, and Horst Rössler, eds. *Distant Magnets: Expectations and Realities in the Immigrant Experience, 1840-1930.* New York: Holmes & Meier, 1993.

Lopata, Helena Znaniecka. *Polish Americans.* New Brunswick, N.J.: Transaction Publishers, 1994.

Ostergren, Robert Clifford. *A Community Transplanted: The Trans-Atlantic Experience of a Swedish Immigrant Settlement in the Upper Middle West, 1835-1915.* Madison, Wis.: University of Wisconsin Press, 1988.

Shaw, Stephen Joseph. *The Catholic Parish as a Way-Station of Ethnicity and Americanization: Chicago's Germans and Italians, 1903-1939.* Brooklyn, N.Y.: Carlson Pub., 1991.

Stolarik, M. Mark. *Immigration and Urbanization: The Slovak Experience, 1870-1918.* New York: AMS Press, 1989.

Vecoli, Rudolph J., and Suzanne M. Sinke, eds. *A Century of European Migrations, 1830-1930.* Urbana, Ill.: University of Illinois Press, 1991.

Walch, Timothy, ed. *Immigrant America: European Ethnicity in the United States.* New York: Garland Publishing Co., 1994.

Americans from the Middle East

Bakalian, Anny P. *Armenian-Americans: From Being to Feeling Armenian.* New Brunswick, N.J.: Transaction Publishers, 1993.

Haddad, Yvonne Yazbeck, and Adair T. Lummis. *Islamic Values in the United States: A Comparative Study.* New York: Oxford University Press, 1987.

Moskos, Charles C. *Greek Americans, Struggle and Success.* New Brunswick, N.J.: Transaction Publishers, 1989.

Naff, Alixa. *Becoming American: The Early Arab Immigrant Experience.* Carbondale, Ill.: Southern Illinois University Press, 1985.

Pilibosian, Khachadoor. *They Called Me Mustafa: Memoir of an Immigrant.* Watertown, Mass.: Ohan Press, 1992.

Saliba, Najib E. *Emigration From Syria and the Syrian-Lebanese Community of*

Worcester, MA. Ligonier, Penn.: Antakya Press, 1992.

Americans from the 'New World'

Bryce-Laporte, Roy S. *Caribbean Immigrations and Their Implications for the United States.* Washington, D.C.: Latin American Program, Woodrow Wilson International Center for Scholars, 1985.

Fitzpatrick, Joseph P. *Puerto Rican Americans: The Meaning of Migration to the Mainland.* Englewood Cliffs, N.J.: Prentice-Hall, 1987.

Gmelch, George, interviewer. *Double Passage: The Lives of Caribbean Migrants Abroad and Back Home.* Ann Arbor, Mich.: University of Michigan Press, 1992.

Heer, David M. *Undocumented Mexicans in the United States.* New York: Cambridge University Press, 1990.

Pachon, Harry, and Louis De Sipio. *New Americans by Choice: Political Perspectives of Latino Immigrants.* Boulder, Col.: Westview Press, 1994.

Portes, Alejandro, and Robert L. Bach. *Latin Journey: Cuban and Mexican Immigrants in the United States.* Berkeley, Calif.: University of California Press, 1985.

Siems, Larry, ed. *Between the Lines: Letters Between Undocumented Mexican and Central American Immigrants and Their Families and Friends.* Hopewell, N.J. : Ecco Press, 1992.

Young, Robert M. *Alambrista! = The Illegal!* [videorecording] New York: Du Art Studio, 1988.

NATIVE AMERICANS

Axtell, James. *The Invasion Within: the Contest of Cultures in Colonial North America*. New York: Oxford University Press, 1985.

Clifton, James A., ed. *Being and Becoming Indian: Biographical Studies of North American Frontiers*. Chicago, Ill.: Dorsey Press, 1989.

Coleman, Michael C. *American Indian Children at School, 1850-1930*. Jackson, Miss.: University Press of Mississippi, 1993.

Cotter, Carol, producer. *Winds of Change: A Matter of Choice*. [videorecording] Alexandria, Va.: PBS Video, 1990.

Hoxie, Frederick E. *A Final Promise: The Campaign to Assimilate the Indians, 1880-1920*. New York: Cambridge Univer-sity Press, 1989.

McLoughlin, William Gerald. *The Cherokees and Christianity, 1794-1870: Essays on Acculturation and Cultural Persis-tence*. Athens, Ga.: University of Geor-gia Press, 1994.

Milanich, Jerald T., and Samuel Proc-tor, eds. *Tacachale: Essays on the Indians of Florida and Southeastern Georgia During the Historic Period*. Gainesville, Fla.: University Press of Florida, 1994.

Unrau, William E. *Mixed-Bloods and Tribal Dissolution: Charles Curtis and the Quest for Indian Identity*. Lawrence, Kan.: University Press of Kansas, 1989.

AMERICANS WHO ARE ALSO FEMALE

Gabaccia, Donna, ed. *Seeking Common Ground: Multidisciplinary Studies of Immi-grant Women in the United States*. Westport, Conn.: Greenwood Press, 1992.

Glenn, Susan Anita. *Daughters of the Shtetl: Life and Labor in the Immigrant Generation*. Ithaca, N.Y.: Cornell University Press, 1990.

National Women's History Project. *Adelante, Mujeres!* [videorecording] Windsor, Calif.: National Women's History Project, 1992.

Nolan, Janet. *Ourselves Alone: Women's Emigration From Ireland, 1885-1920*. Lexington, Ky.: University Press of Kentucky, 1989.

AMERICANS WHO ARE ALSO JEWISH

Barkai, Avraham. *Branching Out: German-Jewish Immigration to the Unit-ed States, 1820-1914*. New York: Holmes & Meier, 1994.

Cowan, Neil M., and Ruth Schwartz Cowan. *Our Parents' Lives: The Ameri-canization of Eastern European Jews*. New York: Basic Books, 1989.

Feingold, Henry L. *A Time for Search-ing: Entering the Mainstream, 1920-1945*. Baltimore, Md.: Johns Hopkins University Press, 1992.

Perlman, Robert. *Bridging Three Worlds: Hungarian-Jewish Americans, 1848-1914*. Amherst, Mass.: Univer-sity of Massachusetts Press, 1991.

Shapiro, Edward S. *A Time for Heal-ing: American Jewry Since World War II*. Baltimore, Md.: Johns Hopkins University Press, 1992.

Sorin, Gerald. *A Time for Building: the Third Migration, 1880-1920*. Balti-more, Md.: Johns Hopkins University Press, 1992.

GEOGRAPHIC REGIONS

EASTERN STATES

Bookbinder, Bernie. *City of the World: New York and Its People*. New York: H. N. Abrams, 1989.

Clark, Dennis. *The Irish in Pennsylva-nia: A People Share a Commonwealth*. University Park, Penn.: Pennsylvania Historical Association, 1991.

Cohen, David Steven, ed. *America, the Dream of My Life: Selections From the Federal Writers' Project's New Jersey Ethnic Survey*. New Brunswick, N.J.: Rutgers University Press, 1990.

Eisenberg, Ellen. *Jewish Agricultural Colonies in New Jersey, 1882-1920*. Syra-cuse, N.Y.: Syracuse University Press, 1995.

Gedmintas, Aleksandras. *An Interesting Bit of Identity: The Dynamics of Ethnic Identity in a Lithuanian-American Com-munity*. New York: AMS Press, 1989.

Gerber, David A. *The Making of an American Pluralism: Buffalo, New York, 1825-60*. Urbana, Ill.: University of Illinois Press, 1989.

Golden, Hilda H. *Immigrant and Native Families: The Impact of Immigration on the Demographic Transformation of West-ern Massachusetts, 1850-1900*. Lanham, Md.: University Press of America, 1994.

Green, Charles St. Clair, and Basil Wilson. *The Struggle for Black Empower-ment in New York City: Beyond the Poli-*

tics of Pigmentation. New York: Praeger, 1989.

Ianni, Francis A. J. *The Acculturation of the Italo-Americans in Norristown, Pennsylvania, 1900-1950.* New York: AMS Press, 1991.

Liptak, Dolores Ann. *European Immigrants and the Catholic Church in Connecticut, 1870-1920.* New York: Center for Migration Studies, 1987.

Lowenstein, Steven M. *Frankfurt on the Hudson: The German-Jewish Community of Washington Heights, 1933-1983, its structure and culture.* Detroit, Mich.: Wayne State University Press, 1989.

Pencak, William, Selma Berrol, and Randall M. Miller, eds. *Immigration to New York.* Philadelphia, Penn.: Balch Institute Press, 1991.

Ridge, John T. *Sligo in New York: The Irish From County Sligo, 1849-1991.* New York: County Sligo Social & Benevolent Association, 1991.

Schwartz, Sally. *"A Mixed Multitude": The Struggle for Toleration in Colonial Pennsylvania.* New York: New York University Press, 1988.

Shaw, Douglas V. *Immigration and Ethnicity in New Jersey History.* Trenton, N.J.: New Jersey Historical Commission, Dept. of State, 1994.

Winnick, Louis. *New People in Old Neighborhoods: The Role of New Immigrants in Rejuvenating New York's Communities.* New York: Russell Sage Foundation, 1990.

South and Southwestern States

Boone, Margaret S. *Capital Cubans: Refugee Adaptation in Washington, D.C.* New York: AMS Press, 1989.

Burns, Allan F. *Maya in Exile: Guatemalans in Florida.* Philadelphia, Penn.: Temple University Press, 1993.

Foley, Douglas E. *Learning Capitalist Culture: Deep in the Heart of Tejas.* Philadelphia, Penn.: University of Pennsylvania Press, 1990.

Gonzales, Manuel G. *The Hispanic Elite of the Southwest.* El Paso, Tex.: University of Texas at El Paso, 1989.

Jones, George Fenwick. *The Georgia Dutch: From the Rhine and Danube to the Savannah, 1733-1783.* Athens, Ga.: University of Georgia Press, 1992.

Maril, Robert Lee. *Living on the Edge of America: At Home on the Texas-Mexico Border.* College Station, Tex.: Texas A & M University Press, 1992.

Mormino, Gary Ross, and George E. Pozzetta. *The Immigrant World of Ybor City: Italians and Their Latin Neighbors in Tampa, 1885-1985.* Urbana, Ill.: University of Illinois Press, 1987.

Portes, Alejandro, and Alex Stepick. *City on the Edge: The Transformation of Miami.* Berkeley, Calif.: University of California Press, 1993.

Walls, Thomas K. *The Japanese Texans.* San Antonio, Tex.: University of Texas Institute of Texan Cultures at San Antonio, 1987.

Middle States

Bernardi, Adria. *Houses with Names: Italian Immigrants of Highwood, Illinois.* Urbana, Ill.: University of Illinois Press, 1990.

Kamphoefner, Walter D. *The Westfalians: From Germany to Missouri.*

Princeton, N.J.: Princeton University Press, 1987.

Lissak, Rivka Shpak. *Pluralism & Progressives: Hull House and the New Immigrants, 1890-1919.* Chicago, Ill.: University of Chicago Press, 1989.

Malik, Iftikhar Haider. *Pakistanis in Michigan: A Study of Third [sic] Culture and Acculteration [sic].* New York: AMS Press, 1989.

Marshall, Marguerite Mitchell. *An Account of Afro-Americans in Southeast Kansas, 1884-1984.* Manhattan, Kan.: Sunflower University Press, 1986.

McQuillan, D. Aidan. *Prevailing Over Time: Ethnic Adjustment on the Kansas Prairies, 1875-1925.* Lincoln, Neb.: University of Nebraska Press, 1990

Muzny, Charles C. *The Vietnamese in Oklahoma City: A Study in Ethnic Change.* New York: AMS Press, 1989.

Padilla, Felix M. *Latino Ethnic Consciousness: The Case of Mexican Americans and Puerto Ricans in Chicago.* Notre Dame, Ind.: University of Notre Dame Press, 1985.

Sletto, Kathryn A. *Douglas County's Immigrants: From Europe to America.* Alexandria, Minn.: Explorer, 1992.

Western States

Baskauskas, Liucija. *An Urban Enclave: Lithuanian Refugees in Los Angeles.* New York: AMS Press, 1985.

Drucker, Philip. *The Native Brotherhoods: Modern Intertribal Organizations on the Northwest Coast.* Brighton, Mich.: Native American Book Publishers, 1991.

Emmons, David M. *The Butte Irish: Class and Ethnicity in an American Mining Town, 1875-1925.* Urbana, Ill.: University of Illinois Press, 1989.

Kwik, Greta. *The Indos in Southern California.* New York: AMS Press, 1989.

Lapp, Rudolph M. *Afro-Americans in California.* San Francisco, Calif.: Boyd & Fraser Pub. Co., 1987.

Leonard, Karen Isaksen. *Making Ethnic Choices: California's Punjabi Mexican Americans.* Philadelphia, Penn.: Temple University Press, 1992.

McCarthy, Kevin F., and R. Burciaza Valdez. *Current and Future Effects of Mexican Immigration in California.* Santa Monica, Calif.: Rand Corp., 1986.

Ong, Paul M., Edna Bonacich, and Lucie Cheng, eds. *The New Asian Immigration in Los Angeles and Global Restructuring.* Philadelphia, Penn.: Temple University Press, 1994.

Overstreet, Everett Louis. *Black on a Background of White: A Chronicle of Afro-Americans' Involvement in America's Last Frontier, Alaska.* Fairbanks, Alaska: Alaska Black Caucus, 1988.

Patterson, George James. *The Unassimilated Greeks of Denver.* New York: AMS Press, 1989.

Rischin, Moses, and John Livingston, eds. *Jews of the American West.* Detroit, Mich.: Wayne State University Press, 1991.

Sensi Isolani, Paola A., and Phylis Cancilla Martinelli, eds. *Struggle and Success: An Anthology of the Italian Immigrant Experience in California.* New York: Center for Migration Studies, 1992.

Social and Cultural Evolution

Multicultural Nation

Abalos, David T. *Latinos in the United States: The Sacred and the Political.* Notre Dame, Ind.: University of Notre Dame Press, 1986.

Abrash, Barbara, and Catherine Egan, eds. *Mediating History: The MAP Guide to Independent Video By and About African American, Asian American, Latino, and Native American People.* New York: New York University Press, 1992.

Alba, Richard D. *Ethnic Identity: The Transformation of White America.* New Haven, Conn.: Yale University Press, 1990.

Auerbach, Susan, ed. *Encyclopedia of Multiculturalism.* New York: Marshall Cavendish, 1994.

Bell, Derrick A. *Faces at the Bottom of the Well: The Permanence of Racism.* New York: Basic Books, 1992.

Buenker, John D., and Lorman A. Ratner, eds. *Multiculturalism in the United States: A Comparative Guide to Acculturation and Ethnicity.* New York: Greenwood Press, 1992.

Chavez, Linda. *Out of the Barrio: Toward a New Politics of Hispanic Assimilation.* New York: Basic Books, 1991.

Cose, Ellis. *A Nation of Strangers: Prejudice, Politics, and the Populating of America.* New York: Morrow, 1992.

Cuellar, Linda. *Biculturalism and Acculturation Among Latinos.* [video-

recording] Princeton, N.J.: Films for the Humanities & Sciences, 1991.

D'Innocenzo, Michael, and Josef P. Sirefman, eds. *Immigration and Ethnicity: American Society — "Melting Pot" or "Salad Bowl"?* New York: Greenwood Press, 1992.

Dinnerstein, Leonard, Roger L. Nichols, and David M. Reimers. *Natives and Strangers: Blacks, Indians, and Immigrants in America.* New York: Oxford University Press, 1990.

Early, Gerald Lyn, ed. *Lure and Loathing: Essays on Race, Identity, and the Ambivalence of Assimilation.* New York: A. Lane/Penguin Press, 1993.

Espiritu, Yen Le. *Asian American Panethnicity: Bridging Institutions and Identities.* Philadelphia, Penn.: Temple University Press, 1992.

Feagin, Joe R., and Hernán Vera. *White Racism: The Basics.* New York: Routledge, 1995.

Foner, Philip Sheldon, and Daniel Rosenberg, eds. *Racism, Dissent, and Asian Americans from 1850 to the Present: A Documentary History.* Westport, Conn.: Greenwood Press, 1993.

Gonzalez, Nancie L., and Carolyn S. McCommon, eds. *Conflict, Migration, and the Expression of Ethnicity.* Boulder, Col.: Westview Press, 1989.

Harles, John C. *Politics in the Lifeboat: Immigrants and the American Democratic Order.* Boulder, Col.: Westview Press, 1993.

Heinze, Andrew R. *Adapting to Abundance: Jewish Immigrants, Mass Consumption, and the Search for American Identity.*

New York: Columbia University Press, 1990.

Higham, John. *Strangers in the Land: Patterns of American Nativism, 1860-1925.* New Brunswick, N.J.: Rutgers University Press, 1988.

Jasso, Guillermina, and Mark R. Rosenzweig. *The New Chosen People: Immigrants in the United States.* New York: Russell Sage Foundation, 1990.

Keefe, Susan E., and Amado M. Padilla. *Chicano Ethnicity.* Albuquerque, N.M.: University of New Mexico Press, 1987.

Kendis, Kaoru Oguri. *A Matter of Comfort: Ethnic Maintenance and Ethnic Style Among Third-Generation Japanese Americans.* New York: AMS Press, 1989.

Krau, Edgar. *The Contradictory Immigrant Problem: A Sociopsychological Analysis.* New York: P. Lang, 1991.

Lacey, Dan. *The Essential Immigrant.* New York: Hippocrene Books, 1990.

Lee, Leo, producer. *The Japanese-American, Four Generations of Adaptation.* [sound recording] Washington, D.C.: National Public Radio, 1979.

Lippard, Lucy R. *Mixed Blessings: New Art in a Multicultural America.* New York: Pantheon Books, 1990.

Mangiafico, Luciano. *Contemporary American Immigrants: Patterns of Filipino, Korean, and Chinese Settlement in the United States.* New York: Praeger, 1988.

Myers, Ernest R., ed. *Challenges for a Changing America: Perspectives on Immi-gration and Multiculturalism in the United States.* San Francisco, Calif.: Austin & Winfield, 1993.

Perin, Constance. *Belonging in America: Reading Between the Lines.* Madison, Wis.: University of Wisconsin Press, 1988.

Ringer, Benjamin B., and Elinor R. Lawless. *Race-Ethnicity and Society.* New York: Routledge, 1989.

Stern, Stephen, and John Allan Cicala, eds. *Creative Ethnicity: Symbols and Strategies of Contemporary Ethnic Life.* Logan, Utah: Utah State University Press, 1991.

Szasz, Margaret, ed. *Between Indian and White Worlds: The Cultural Broker.* Norman, Okla.: University of Oklahoma Press, 1994.

Takaki, Ronald T. *A Different Mirror: A History of Multicultural America.* Boston, Mass.: Little, Brown, 1993.

Takaki, Ronald T. *Iron Cages: Race and Culture in 19th-Century America.* New York: Oxford University Press, 1990.

Tollefson, James W. *Alien Winds: The Reeducation [sic] of America's Indochinese Refugees.* New York: Praeger, 1989.

Trueba, Henry T., Lila Jacobs, and Elizabeth Kirton. *Cultural Conflict and Adaptation: The Case of Hmong Children in American Society.* New York: Falmer Press, 1990.

Warehime, Nancy. *To Be One of Us: Cultural Conflict, Creative Democracy, and Education.* Albany, N.Y.: State University of New York Press, 1993.

Wei, William. *The Asian American Movement.* Philadelphia, Penn.: Temple University Press, 1993.

Wellman, David T. *Portraits of White Racism.* New York: Cambridge University Press, 1993.

Weyr, Thomas. *Hispanic U.S.A.: Breaking the Melting Pot.* New York: Harper & Row, 1988.

Whittaker, Elvi W. *The Mainland Haole: The White Experience in Hawaii.* New York: Columbia University Press, 1986.

Wyszkowski, Charles. *A Community in Conflict: American Jewry During the Great European Immigration.* Lanham, Md.: University Press of America, 1991.

Yinger, J. Milton. *Ethnicity: Source of Strength? Source of Conflict?* Albany, N.Y.: State University of New York Press, 1994.

REFUGEES AND THEIR IMPACT

Baumel, Judith Tydor. *Unfulfilled Promise: Rescue and Resettlement of Jewish Refugee Children in the United States, 1934-1945.* Juneau, Alaska: Denali Press, 1990.

Coser, Lewis A. *Refugee Scholars in America: Their Impact and Their Experiences.* New Haven, Conn.: Yale University Press, 1984.

De Zayas, Alfred M. *The German Expellees: Victims in War and Peace.* New York: St. Martin's Press, 1993.

Haines, David W., ed. *Refugees as Immigrants: Cambodians, Laotians, and Vietnamese in America.* Totowa, N.J.: Rowman & Littlefield, 1989.

Heilbut, Anthony. *Exiled in Paradise: German Refugee Artists and Intellectuals in America, from the 1930s to the Present.* New York: Viking Press, 1983.

Lehmann, Hartmut, and James J. Sheehan, eds. *An Interrupted Past: German-Speaking Refugee Historians in the United States After 1933.* New York: Cambridge University Press, 1991.

Maga, Timothy P. *America, France, and the European Refugee Problem, 1933-1947.* New York: Garland Publishing Co., 1985.

Mann, Erika, and Klaus Mann. *Escape to Life.* Munchen, Ger.: Spangenberg, 1991.

Merrill-Mirsky, Carol, ed. *Exiles in Paradise.* Los Angeles, Calif.: Los Angeles Philharmonic Association, 1991.

Nettelbeck, Colin W. *Forever French: Exile in the United States, 1939-1945.* New York: Berg, 1991.

Peck, Abraham J., ed. *The German-Jewish Legacy in America, 1938-1988: From Bildung to the Bill of Rights.* Detroit, Mich.: Wayne State University Press, 1989.

Simpson, Christopher. *Blowback: America's Recruitment of Nazis and its Effects on the Cold War.* New York: Collier Books, 1989.

PERCEPTIONS OF THE IMMIGRANT

Lambert, Wallace E., and Donald M. Taylor. *Coping with Cultural and Racial Diversity in Urban America.* New York: Praeger, 1990.

Muller, Thomas et al. *The Fourth Wave: California's Newest Immigrants.* Washington, D.C.: Urban Institute Press, 1985.

O'Neill, Teresa. *Immigration: Opposing Viewpoints.* San Diego, Calif.: Greenhaven Press, 1992.

Okihiro, Gary Y. *Cane Fires: The Anti-Japanese Movement in Hawaii, 1865-1945.* Philadelphia, Penn.: Temple University Press, 1991.

Richard, Alfred Charles. *The Hispanic Image on the Silver Screen: An Interpretive Filmography from Silents into Sound, 1898-1935.* New York: Greenwood Press, 1992.

Roper Organization. *American Attitudes Toward Immigration.* [United States]: Roper Organization, 1992.

Simon, Rita James, and Susan H. Alexander. *The Ambivalent Welcome: Print Media, Public Opinion, and Immigration.* Westport, Conn.: Praeger, 1993.

Sutter, Valerie O'Connor. *The Indochinese Refugee Dilemma.* Baton Rouge, La.: Louisiana State University Press, 1990.

Thatcher, Mary Anne. *Immigrants and the 1930s: Ethnicity and Alienage in Depression and On-Coming War.* New York: Garland Publishing Co., 1990.

Toplin, Robert Brent, ed. *Hollywood as Mirror: Changing Views of "Outsiders" and "Enemies" in American Movies.* Westwood, Conn.: Greenwood Press, 1993.

Trager, Oliver, ed. *America's Minorities and the Multicultural Debate.* New York: Facts on File, 1992.

JUVENILE

JUVENILE, FICTION

Atlas, Susan. *The Passover Passage.* Los Angeles, Calif.: Torah Aura Productions, 1989.

Bartoletti, Susan Campbell. *Silver at Night.* New York: Crown, 1994.

Benson, Rita. *Rosa's Diary.* Santa Rosa, Calif.: SRA, 1994.

Conlon-McKenna, Marita. *Wildflower Girl.* New York: Puffin Books, 1994.

Douglas, Marjory Stoneman. *Freedom River.* Miami, Fla.: Valiant Press, 1994.

Garaway, Margaret Kahn. *Ashkii (Ashkey), and His Grandfather.* Tucson, Ariz.: Treasure Chest Publications, 1989.

Gilmore, Rachna. *Lights for Gita.* Gardiner, Maine: Tilbury House, 1995.

Gross, Virginia T. *It's Only Goodbye.* New York: Puffin Books, 1992.

Hanson, Regina. *Tangerine Tree.* New York: Clarion Books, 1995.

Hart, Jan Siegel. *Many Adventures of Minnie.* Austin, Tex.: Eakin Press, 1992.

Hesse, Karen. *Letters From Rifka.* New York: H. Holt, 1992.

Hoff, Carol. *Johnny Texas.* Dallas, Tex.: Hendrick-Long, 1992.

Hughes, Langston. *Black Misery.* New York: Oxford University Press, 1994.

Kavanagh, Katie. *Home is Where Your Family Is.* Austin, Tex.: Raintree Steck-Vaughn, 1994.

Levine, Ellen. *I Hate English!* New York: Scholastic, 1991.

Levinson, Riki. *Soon, Annala.* New York: Orchard Books, 1993.

Levitin, Sonia. *A Piece of Home*. New York: Dial Books for Young Readers, 1995.

Mohr, Nicholasa. *The Magic Shell*. New York: Scholastic, 1995.

Moss, Marissa. *In America*. New York: Dutton Children's Books, 1994.

Munson, Sammye. *Goodbye, Sweden, Hello Texas*. Austin, Tex.: Eakin Press, 1994.

Nixon, Joan Lowery. *Land of Dreams*. New York: Delacorte Press, 1994.

Roseman, Kenneth. *The Other Side of the Hudson: A Jewish Immigrant Adventure*. New York: UAHC, 1993.

Ross, Lillian Hammer. *Sarah, Also Known as Hannah*. Morton Grove, Ill.: A. Whitman, 1994.

Shiefman, Vicky. *Good-bye to the Trees*. New York: Atheneum, 1993.

St. Hill, Harriett L. *My Name, Nkili, Tells Me I'm Beautiful: N-ke-le*. Brooklyn, N.Y.: Books Unlimited, 1989.

Tawa, Mana. *When Hopi Children Were Bad: A Monster Story*. Sacramento, Calif.: Sierra Oaks Pub. Co., 1989.

Wheeler, Jill C. *Wolf of the Desert: The Story of Geronimo*. Bloomington, Minn.: Abdo & Daughters, 1989.

JUVENILE, NON-FICTION

Anderson, Kelly C. *Immigration*. San Diego, Calif.: Lucent Books, 1993.

Andryszewski, Tricia. *Immigration: Newcomers and Their Impact on the U.S.*

Brookfield, Conn.: Millbrook Press, 1995.

Andryszewski, Tricia. *The Seminoles: People of the Southeast*. Brookfield, Conn.: Millbrook Press, 1995.

Ashabranner, Brent K. *Still a Nation of Immigrants*. New York: Cobblehill Books/Dutton, 1993.

Bales, Carol Ann. *Tales of the Elders: A Memory Book of Men and Women Who Came to America as Immigrants, 1900-1930*. Morristown, N.J.: Silver Burdett Press, 1993.

Bandon, Alexandra. *Filipino Americans*. New York: New Discovery Books, 1993.

Berger, Melvin, and Gilda Berger. *Where Did Your Family Come From?: A Book About Immigrants*. Nashville, Tenn.: Ideals Children's Books, 1993.

Bode, Janet. *New Kids on the Block: Oral Histories of Immigrant Teens*. New York: F. Watts, 1989.

Bouvier, Leon F. *Think About Immigration: Social Diversity in the U.S.* New York: Walker, 1992.

Bratman, Fred. *Becoming a Citizen: Adopting a New Home*. Austin, Tex.: Raintree Steck-Vaughn, 1993.

Bresnick-Perry, Roslyn. *Leaving for America*, San Francisco, Calif.: Children's Book Press, 1992.

Caroli, Betty Boyd. *Immigrants Who Returned Home*. New York: Chelsea House, 1990.

Dawson, Mildred Leinweber. *Over Here It's Different: Carolina's Story*. New York: Macmillan, 1993.

Evitts, William J. *Early Immigration in the United States*. New York: F. Watts, 1989.

Fassler, David, and Kimberly Danforth. *Coming to America: The Kids' Book About Immigration*. Burlington, Vt.: Waterfront, 1993.

Giovanni, Nikki. *Spin a Soft Black Song: Poems for Children*. New York: Hill and Wang, 1985.

Goldfish, Meish. *Immigration: How Should It Be Controlled?* New York: Twenty-First Century Books, 1994.

Gordon, Ginger. *My Two Worlds*. New York: Clarion Books, 1993.

Gordon, Susan. *Asian Indians*. New York: F. Watts, 1990.

Grenquist, Barbara. *Cubans*. New York: F. Watts, 1991.

Hamanaka, Sheila. *The Journey: Japanese Americans, Racism, and Renewal*. New York: Orchard Books, 1990.

Hauser, Pierre N. *Illegal Aliens*. New York: Chelsea House, 1990.

Herda, D. J. *Ethnic America: The South Central States*. Brookfield, Conn.: Millbrook Press, 1991.

Hillbrand, Percie V. *The Norwegians in America*. Minneapolis, Minn.: Lerner Publications Co., 1991.

Howlett, Bud. *I'm New Here*. Boston, Mass.: Houghton Mifflin, 1993.

Hunter, Latoya. *The Diary of Latoya Hunter: My First Year in Junior High*. New York: Crown, 1992.

Jacobs, William Jay. *Ellis Island: New Hope in a New Land.* New York: C. Scribner's, 1990.

Jafferian, Serpoohi Christine. *Winds of Destiny: An Immigrant Girl's Odyssey.* Belmont, Mass.: Armenian Heritage Press, 1993.

Jensen, Jeffry. *Hispanic American Struggle for Equality.* Vero Beach, Fla.: Rourke Corp., 1992.

Jones, Maxine Deloris. *African Americans in Florida.* Sarasota, Fla.: Pineapple Press, 1993.

Katz, William Loren. *The Great Migrations, 1880s-1912.* Austin, Tex: Raintree Steck-Vaughn, 1993.

Knight, Margy Burns. *Who Belongs Here? An American Story.* Gardiner, Maine: Tilbury House, 1993.

Koral, April. *An Album of the Great Wave of Immigration.* New York: F. Watts, 1992.

Kuklin, Susan. *How My Family Lives in America.* New York: Bradbury Press, 1992.

Lakin, Pat. *Everything You Need to Know When a Parent Doesn't Speak English.* New York: Rosen Pub. Group, 1994.

Lee, Kathleen. *Tracing Our Italian Roots.* Santa Fe, N.M.: J. Muir Publications, 1993.

Lee, Kathleen. *Tracing Our Chinese Roots.* Santa Fe, N.M.: J. Muir Publications, 1994.

Levine, Ellen. *If Your Name Was Changed at Ellis Island.* New York: Scholastic, 1993.

Maestro, Betsy. *Coming to America: The Story of Immigration.* New York: Scholastic, 1995.

Mayberry, Jodine. *Eastern Europeans.* New York: F. Watts, 1991.

McGuire, William. *Southeast Asians.* New York: F. Watts, 1991.

Michels, Barbara, ed. *Apples on a Stick: The Folklore of Black Children.* New York: Coward-McCann, 1983.

Moscinski, Sharon. *Tracing Our Polish Roots.* Santa Fe, N.M.: J. Muir Publications, 1994.

O'Connor, Karen. *Dan Thuy's New Life in America.* Minneapolis, Minn.: Lerner Publications Co., 1992.

Poynter, Margaret. *The Uncertain Journey: Stories of Illegal Aliens in El Norte.* New York: Atheneum, 1992.

Reiff, Tana. *Stories of the Immigration Experience.* Belmont, Calif.: Fearon Education, 1989.

Sagan, Miriam. *Tracing Our Jewish Roots.* Santa Fe, N.M.: J. Muir Publications, 1993.

Sandler, Martin W. *Immigrants.* New York: Harper Collins, 1995.

Sonder, Ben. *The Tenement Writer: An Immigrant's Story.* Austin, Tex.: Raintree Steck-Vaughn, 1993.

Szumski, Bonnie. *Immigration: Identifying Propaganda Techniques.* San Diego, Calif.: Greenhaven Press, 1989.

Takaki, Ronald T. *Spacious Dreams: The First Wave of Asian Immigration.* New York: Chelsea House, 1994.

Takaki, Ronald T. *Strangers at the Gates Again: Asian American Immigration After 1965.* New York: Chelsea House, 1995.

JUVENILE, RESOURCES

Anderson, Vicki. *Immigrants in the United States in Fiction: A Guide to 705 Books for Librarians and Teachers, K-9.* Jefferson, N.C.: McFarland, 1994.

Hayden, Carla Diane, ed. *Venture into Cultures: A Resource Book of Multicultural Materials and Programs.* Chicago, Ill.: American Library Association, 1992.

Pilger, Mary Anne. *Multicultural Projects Index: Things to Make and Do to Celebrate Festivals, Cultures, and Holidays Around the World.* Englewood, Col.: Libraries Unlimited, 1992.

Roberts, Patricia L., and Nancy Lee Cecil. *Developing Multicultural Awareness Through Children's Literature: A Guide for Teachers and Librarians, Grades K-8.* Jefferson, N.C.: McFarland, 1993.

CURATORS

CURATORS' RECOMMENDATIONS

Across the Pacific: Contemporary Korean and Korean American Art. Queens, N.Y.: Queens Museum of Art, 1993.

"Culture, Identity, & Colonialism." *WhiteWalls* no. 31 (1992): special issue.

Seven Contemporary Korean-American Visual Artists. Belmont, Calif.: College of the Notre Dame, 1994.

Treasure in the House. Santa Monica, Calif.: Highways, 1991.

WESTAF-NEA Regional Fellowships for Visual Arts. Santa Fe, N.M.: Western States Arts Federation, 1993.

Acuña, Rodolfo. *Occupied America: A History of Chicanos*. New York: Harper & Row, 1981.

Alexander, Stuart. *Robert Frank: A Bibliography, Filmography, and Exhibition Chronology, 1946-1985*. Tucson, Ariz.: Center for Creative Photography, 1986.

Alland, Alexander. *American Counterpoint*. New York: John Day Co., 1943.

Alland, Alexander. *Jacob A. Riis: Photographer & Citizen*. Millerton, N.Y.: Aperture, 1974.

Avery, Virginia. *The Definitive Contemporary American Quilt*. New York: Bernice Steinbaum Gallery, 1990.

Barolini, Helen et al. *Images: A Pictorial History of Italian Americans*. New York: Center for Migration, 1986.

Becker, Carol et al., contributors. *Different Voices: A Social, Cultural, and Historical Framework for Change in the American Art Museum*. New York: Association of Art Museum Directors, 1992.

Black Elk. *Black Elk Speaks: Being the Life Story of a Holy Man of the Oglala Sioux, as Told Through John G. Neihardt*. Lincoln, Neb.: University of Nebraska Press, 1979.

Brown, Dee Alexander. *Bury My Heart at Wounded Knee: An Indian History of the American West*. New York: Holt, Rinehart & Winston, 1971.

Brown, Wesley, and Amy Ling, eds. *Visions of America: Personal Narratives From the Promised Land*. New York: Persea Books, 1993.

Brownstone, David M. *The Irish-American Heritage*. New York: Facts on File, 1989.

Calloway, Colin G., ed. *Dawnland Encounters: Indians and Europeans in Northern New England*. Hanover, N.H.: University Press of New England, 1991.

Cardoso, Lawrence A. *Mexican Emigration to the United States, 1897-1931: Socio-Economic Patterns*. Tucson, Ariz.: University of Arizona Press, 1980.

Chan, Sucheng. *This Bittersweet Soil: the Chinese in California Agriculture, 1860-1910*. Berkeley, Calif.: Univer-sity of California Press, 1986.

Chermayeff, Ivan, designer. *Ellis Island: An Illustrated History of the Immigrant Experience*. New York: Macmillan, 1991.

Chong, Albert. *Ancestral Dialogues: The Photographs of Albert Chong*. San Francisco, Calif.: The Friends of Photography, 1994.

Cohen, Lucy M. *Chinese in the Post-Civil War South: A People Without a History*. Baton Rouge, La.: Louisiana State University Press, 1984.

Coleman, A. D. "Marion Palfi: My Studio is the World." *Camera & Darkroom* 15, no. 10 (October 1993): 42-51.

Conrat, Maisie, and Richard Conrat. *Executive Order 9066: The Internment of 110,000 Japanese Americans*. Los Ange-les, Calif.: Asian American Studies Center, UCLA, 1992.

Cowan, Neil M., and Ruth Schwartz Cowan. *Our Parents' Lives: The Americanization of Eastern European Jews*. New York: Basic Books, 1989.

Daniels, Roger. *Coming to America: A History of Immigration and Ethnicity in American Life*. New York: Harper Collins, 1990.

Davis, Marilyn P. *Mexican Voices/American Dreams: An Oral History of Mexican Immigration to the United States*. New York: H. Holt, 1990.

Dicker, Laverne Mau. *Chinese in San Francisco: A Pictorial History*. New York: Dover Publications, 1979.

Diner, Hasia R. *Erin's Daughters in America: Irish Immigrant Women in the Nineteenth Century*. Baltimore, Md.: Johns Hopkins University Press, 1983.

Drudy, P. J., ed. *Irish in America: Emigration, Assimilation and Impact*. New York: Cambridge University Press, 1985.

DuBois, Ellen Carol, and Vicki L. Ruiz, eds. *Unequal Sisters: A Multicultural Reader in U.S. Women's History*. New York: Routledge, 1990.

Enyeart, James L. *Invisible in America: An Exhibition of Photographs by Marion Palfi*. Lawrence, Kan.: University of Kansas Museum of Art, 1973.

Ewen, Elizabeth. *Immigrant Women in the Land of Dollars: Life and Culture on the Lower East Side, 1890-1925*. New York: Monthly Review Press, 1985.

Fassler, David, and Kimberly Danforth. *Coming to America: The Kids' Book About Immigration.* Burlington, Vt.: Waterfront, 1993.

Franck, Irene M. *Scandinavian-American Heritage.* New York: Facts on File, 1988.

Frank, Robert. *The Americans.* Millerton, N.Y.: Aperture, 1978.

Frank, Robert. *The Lines of My Hand.* New York: Pantheon, 1989.

Fuchs, Lawrence H. *The American Kaleidoscope: Race, Ethnicity, and the Civic Culture.* Hanover, N.H.: Wesleyan University Press, 1990.

Fuentes, Carlos. *The Buried Mirror: Reflections on Spain and the New World.* Boston, Mass.: Houghton Mifflin, 1992.

Garcia, Mario T. *Mexican Americans: Leadership, Ideology & Identity, 1930-1960.* New Haven, Conn.: Yale University Press, 1989.

Gates, Henry Louis. *Loose Canons: Notes on the Culture Wars.* New York: Oxford University Press, 1992.

Genthe, Arnold. *Genthe's Photographs of San Francisco's Old Chinatown.* New York: Dover Publications, 1984.

Goldblatt, Louis and Otto Hagel. *Men and Machines.* San Francisco, Calif.: International Longshoreman's and Warehouseman's Union, 1963.

Gonzales, Manuel E. *Caught Among the Cultures.* Miami, Fla.: Art Museum of the International University, 1993.

Greenough, Sarah and Philip Brookman. *Robert Frank: Moving Out.* Washington, D.C.: National Gallery of Art, 1994.

Griffin, William D. *The Book of Irish Americans.* New York: Times Books, 1990.

Gudis, Catherine, ed. *LAX, the Los Angeles Exhibition 92.* Los Angeles, Calif.: Directors of the Gallery at Barnsdall Art Park, 1992.

Gutiérrez, Ramón Arturo. *When Jesus Came, the Corn Mothers Went Away: Marriage, Sexuality, and Power in New Mexico, 1500-1846.* Stanford, Calif.: Stanford University Press, 1991.

Gutmann, John. *As I Saw It: Photographs.* San Francisco, Calif.: San Francisco Museum of Modern Art, 1976.

Hertzberg, Arthur. *The Jews in America: Four Centuries of an Uneasy Encounter.* New York: Simon & Schuster, 1989.

Hine, Lewis Wickes. *America & Lewis Hine: Photographs, 1904-1940.* Millerton, N.Y.: Aperture, 1977.

Hirsch, Eric Donald. *Cultural Literacy: What Every American Needs to Know.* Boston, Mass.: Houghton Mifflin, 1987.

Hoffman, Abraham. *Unwanted Mexican Americans in the Great Depression: Repatriation Pressures, 1929-1939.* Tucson, Ariz.: University of Arizona Press, 1974.

Howe, Irving, and Kenneth Libo, eds. *How We Lived: A Documentary History of Immigrant Jews in America, 1880-1930.* New York: R. Marek, 1979.

Howe, Irving. *World of Our Fathers: The Journey of the East European Jews to America and the Life They Found and Made.* New York: Simon & Schuster, 1983.

Hurley, F. Jack. *Russell Lee, Photographer.* Dobbs Ferry, N.Y.: Morgan & Morgan, 1978.

Ichioka, Yuji. *The Issei: The World of the First Generation Japanese Immigrants, 1885-1924.* New York: Free Press, 1988.

In Terms of Time. Santa Barbara, Calif.: Santa Barbara Contemporary Arts Forum, 1994.

Ito, Kazuo. *Issei: A History of Japanese Immigrants in North America.* Seattle, Wash.: Japanese Community Service, 1973.

Jonas, Susan, ed. *Ellis Island: Echoes From a Nation's Past.* New York: Aperture Foundation, 1989.

Kano, Kouichi. *Third International Textile Competition, Kyoto.* Kyoto, Japan: Kyoto Museum of Art, 1992.

Kraut, Alan M. *Silent Travelers: Germs, Genes, and the "Immigrant Menace."* New York: Basic Books, 1994.

Lai, H. Mark, Genny Lim, and Judy Yung, trans. *Island: Poetry and History of Chinese Immigrants on Angel Island, 1910-1940.* San Francisco, Calif.: Hoc Doi, 1980.

Lee, Gavin. *Family.* January 25-February 25, 1993. Woodland Hills, Calif.: Pierce College Art Gallery, 1993.

Lee, Joann Faung Jean. *Asian Americans: Oral Histories of First to Fourth Generation Americans from China, the*

Philippines, Japan, India, the Pacific Islands, Vietnam, and Cambodia. New York: New Press, 1992.

Leong, Russell, ed. *Moving the Image: Independent Asian Pacific American Media Arts.* Los Angeles, Calif.: Asian American Studies Center, UCLA, 1991.

Lindquist-Cock, Elizabeth. *Marion Palfi. Archive* 19. Tucson, Ariz.: Center for Creative Photography, 1983.

Lyman, Stanford M. *Chinatown and Little Tokyo: Power, Conflict, and Community Among Chinese and Japanese Immigrants in America.* Millwood, N.Y.: Associated Faculty Press, 1986.

Marzio, Peter C., ed. *A Nation of Nations: The People Who Came to America as Seen Through Objects and Documents Exhibited at the Smithsonian Institution.* New York: Harper & Row, 1976.

McCunn, Ruthanne Lum. *Chinese American Portraits: Personal Histories, 1828-1988.* San Francisco, Calif.: Chronicle Books, 1988.

Meltzer, Milton. *Dorothea Lange: A Photographer's Life.* New York: Farrar, Straus, Giroux, 1978.

Mieth, Hansel, and Otto Hagel. *The Simple Life: Photographs From America, 1929-1971.* Stuttgart , Ger.: Schmetterling, 1991.

Model, Lisette. *Lisette Model. Archive* 4. Tucson, Ariz.: Center for Creative Photography, 1977.

Model, Lisette. *Lisette Model.* Millerton, N.Y.: Aperture, 1979.

Monroy, Douglas. *Thrown Among Strangers: The Making of Mexican Culture in Frontier California.* Berkeley, Calif.: University of California Press, 1990.

Myers, Walter Dean. *Now Is Your Time!: The African-American Struggle for Freedom.* New York: Harper Collins Children's Books, 1991.

Personal Justice Denied: Report of the Commission on Wartime Relocation and Internment of Civilians. Washington, D.C.: Commission on Wartime Relocation and Internment of Civilians, 1983.

Phillips, Sandra S. *John Gutmann: Beyond the Document.* San Francisco, Calif.: San Francisco Museum of Modern Art, 1989.

Polenberg, Richard. *One Nation Divisible: Class, Race, and Ethnicity in the United States Since 1938.* New York: Viking Press, 1980.

Portes, Alejandro, and Rubén G. Rumbaut. *Immigrant America: A Portrait.* Berkeley, Calif.: University of California Press, 1990.

Reeves, Pamela. *Ellis Island: Gateway to the American Dream.* New York: Dorset Press, 1991.

Riesenberg, Felix and Alexander Alland. *Portrait of New York.* New York: Macmillan, 1939.

Riis, Jacob A. *How the Other Half Lives: Studies Among the Tenements of New York.* New York: Dover, 1971.

Rosenblum, Naomi, and Larry Heinemann. *Changing Chicago: A Photodocumentary.* Urbana, Ill.: University of Illinois Press, 1989.

Sachar, Howard Morley. *A History of the Jews in America.* New York: Knopf, 1992.

Sanders, Ronald. *Shores of Refuge: A Hundred Years of Jewish Emigration.* New York: H. Holt, 1988.

Sarasohn, Eileen Sunada, ed. *The Issei: Portrait of a Pioneer, an Oral History.* Palo Alto, Calif.: Pacific Books, 1983.

Schoener, Allon. *The American Jewish Album: 1654 to the Present.* New York: Rizzoli, 1983.

Schoener, Allon. *The Italian Americans.* New York: MacMillan, 1987.

Schreier, Barbara A. *Becoming American Women: Clothing and the Jewish Immigrant Experience, 1880-1920.* Chicago, Ill.: Chicago Historical Society, 1994.

Simmons, William Scranton. *Spirit of the New England Tribes: Indian History and Folklore, 1620-1984.* Hanover, N.H.: University Press of New England, 1986.

Siu, Paul C. P. *The Chinese Laundryman: A Study of Social Isolation.* New York: New York University Press, 1987.

Sorgenfrei, Robert and David Peters, comp. *Marion Palfi Archive. Guide Series* 10. Tucson, Ariz.: Center for Creative Photography, 1985.

Sowell, Thomas. *The Ethnic America: A History.* New York: Basic Books, 1981.

Steinberg, Stephen. *The Ethnic Myth: Race, Ethnicity, and Class in America.* New York: Atheneum, 1981.

Steltzer, Ulli. *The New Americans: Immigrant Life in Southern California.* Pasadena, Calif.: New Sage Press, 1988.

Sutnik, Maia-Mari. *Gutmann: August 24-October 20, 1985.* Toronto, Ont.: Art Gallery of Ontario, 1985.

Takaki, Ronald T. *A Different Mirror: A History of Multicultural America.* Boston, Mass.: Little, Brown, 1993.

Takaki, Ronald T. *Iron Cages: Race and Culture in 19th-Century America.* New York: Oxford University Press, 1990.

Takaki, Ronald T. *Strangers From a Different Shore: A History of Asian Americans.* Boston, Mass.: Little, Brown, 1989.

Tanaka, Chester. *Go For Broke: A Pictorial History of the Japanese American 100th Infantry Battalion and the 442nd Regimental Combat Team.* Richmond, Calif.: Go For Broke, 1982.

Tateishi, John, comp. *And Justice For All: An Oral History of the Japanese American Detention Camps.* New York: Random House, 1984.

Thomas, Ann. *Lisette Model.* Ottawa, Ont.: National Gallery of Canada, 1990.

Thomas, Lew, ed. *The Restless Decade: John Gutmann's Photographs of the Thirties.* New York: H. N. Abrams, 1984.

Tucker, Anne Wilkes. *Robert Frank: New York to Nova Scotia.* Boston, Mass.: Little, Brown, 1986.

Wakatsuki, Yasno. "Japanese Emigration to the United States, 1866-1924."

Perspectives in American History 12 (1979): 387-516.

Walker, Scott, ed. *Stories From the American Mosaic.* Saint Paul, Minn.: Graywolf Press, 1990.

Webb, Alex. *Hot Light/Half-Made Worlds: Photographs From the Tropics.* New York: Thames and Hudson, 1986.

Webb, Alex. *Under a Grudging Sun: Photographs From Haiti Libéré, 1986-1988.* New York: Thames and Hudson, 1989.

Weber, David J., ed. *Foreigners in Their Native Land: Historical Roots of the Mexican Americans.* Albuquerque, N.M.: University of New Mexico Press, 1973.

Wilson, Robert Arden, and Bill Hasokawa. *East to America: A History of the Japanese in the United States.* New York: Morrow, 1980.

Wolfman, Ira. *Do People Grow on Family Trees? Genealogy For Kids & Other Beginners: The Official Ellis Island Handbook.* New York: Workman Publishing Co., 1991.

Yochelson, Bonnie. *The Committed Eye: Alexander Alland's Photography.* New York: Museum of the City of New York, 1991.

Ziff, Trisha, ed. *Between Worlds: Contemporary Mexican Photography.* New York: Institute of Contemporary Photography, 1990.

Zinn, Howard. *People's History of the United States.* New York: Harper & Row, 1980.

1   F. Bartolozzi, after Benjamin West, *An Indian Cacique of the Island of Cuba, addressing Columbus concerning a future state*, 1794. Wood engraving, 7¾ by 6½ in. Courtesy Chicago Historical Society

2   Unknown artist, Untitled (cutaway sectional renderings of slave ship), 1808, printed later. Gelatin silver print of wood engraving, 8 by 10 in. Courtesy Prints and Photographs Division, Library of Congress, Washington DC

3   H. Teape & Son, London (printer), *"Rules and Regulations For Steerage Passengers,"* c. 1820. Printed text, 14¼ by 12 in. Courtesy Chicago Historical Society

4   C. J. Grant, *"Emigration, Detailing the Progress and Vicissitudes of an Emigrant!"*, 1833. Lithograph, 14 by 10⁵/₁₆ in. Courtesy Prints and Photographs Division, Library of Congress, Washington DC

5   William Shew, American, 1820–1903, *Gold mining with Chinese workers*, c. 1850. Daguerreotype, 4¼ by 5¼ in. Courtesy The Stanley B. Burns, M.D. Collection

6   Napoleon Sarony, American, b. Canada, 1821–1896, *Photographer, Self-portrait*, c. 1860s. Albumen silver print, 3⅞ by 2¼ in. Courtesy Janet Lehr, Inc. New York

7   Unknown artist, Untitled (John Hillers, photographer, on right), c. 1860s. Albumen silver print, right half of stereograph, 4¼ by 6 in. Courtesy Janet Lehr, Inc., New York

8   James Wallace Black, American, 1825–1896, *Louis Agassiz, 1807–1873, Swiss-born American naturalist*, c. 1860s. Albumen silver print, 3⅝ by 2⅛ in. Collection Museum of Photographic Arts, Museum purchase

9   James Wallace Black, American, 1825–1896, *Carl Schurz, Secretary of Interior*, c. 1860s. Albumen silver print, 3¾ by 2¼ in. Collection Museum of Photographic Arts, Museum purchase

10   Unknown artist, *"Beware of Foreign Influence!"*, 1850. Printed text with engraving, 24 by 18¾ in. Courtesy Chicago Historical Society

11   Rufus Anson, American, active 1851–1867, *Rebecca Jackson Noah (Mrs. Mordecai Manuel), born England (1810–1866)*, c. 1850s. Daguerreotype, 2¾ by 2¼ in. Courtesy American Jewish Historical Society, Waltham, Massachusetts

12   Unknown artist, *Mrs. Isaac Phillips (Sophia), born England, (1810–1855)*, c. 1850s. Daguerreotype, 2¾ by 2¼ in. Courtesy American Jewish Historical Society, Waltham, Massachusetts

13   Eadweard J. Muybridge, American, b. Britain, 1830–1904, *The 'Heathen Chinee' with pick and rocker*, 1868–1872. Stereograph, 3¾ by 6³/₁₆ in. Courtesy California Historical Society, San Francisco (FN-13890)

14   G. R. Hall, after Alonzo Chappel, *Landing of Roger Williams*, 1857. Wood engraving, 5¾ by 7½ in. Courtesy Chicago Historical Society

15   Unknown artist, *"Slave Deck of the Bark 'Wildfire', Brought into Key West on April 30, 1860,"* from *Harper's Weekly*, July 6, 1860. Wood engraving, 16¼ by 11¼ in. Courtesy Collection Lower East Side Tenement Museum

16   Unknown artist, *Officers of the Irish Brigade at Mass in camp in Northern Virginia*, 1864, printed later. Gelatin silver print, 8 by 10 in. Courtesy Prints and Photographs Division, Library of Congress, Washington DC

17   Alfred A. Hart, American, 1816–1908, *Railroad construction at Secrettown, Sierra Nevada*, c. 1868. Albumen silver print, 7½ by 9⅜ in. Courtesy The Bancroft Library

18   T. Thulstrup, after C. A. Booth, *"The Massacre of the Chinese at Rock Springs, Wyoming,"* from *Harpers Weekly*, September 26, 1885, vol.29, no.1501, p. 637. Wood engraving, 9¹/₁₆ by 14 in. Courtesy Fales Library, New York Uni-

versity (for exhibition loan); Courtesy The Bancroft Library (for reproduction permission)

19   Unknown artist, *400,000 New Acres* (broadside, issued by St. Paul, Minneapolis and Manitoba Realty Company), c. 1870. Printed text, 21¾ by 8 in. Courtesy Minnesota Historical Society Collections, Great Northern Railway Company Archives

20   Unknown artist, *Shakespeare, A Jamaican Negro*, c. 1870. Tintype, full plate, 7⅜ by 5³/₁₆ in. Courtesy Historic New Orleans Collection (1965.90.268.3)

21   Unknown artist, *"Cost of Coming to Minnesota,"* (broadside, issued by the Secretary of the State Board of Immigration), c. 1872. Printed text, 9 by 4½ in. Courtesy Minnesota Historical Society Collections, Great Northern Railway Company Archives

22   Unknown artist, Untitled (Chinese roadbuilders), c. 1875. Albumen silver print, 6¼ by 7¹⁵/₁₆ in. Courtesy The Sara Cleary-Burns Collection

23   Andreas Larsen Dahl, American, b. Norway, 1844–1923, *Siri Rustebakke, center, with daughters and daughter-in-law, Town of Black Earth, Wisconsin*, c. 1873, printed later. Gelatin silver print from glass plate negative, 8 by 10 in. Courtesy State Historical Society of Wisconsin (Whi D31 260)

24   Andreas Larsen Dahl, American, b. Norway, 1844–1923, *Lars Davidson Reque, frame house and family*, 1874, printed later. Gelatin silver print from original glass plate negative, 8 by 10 in. Courtesy State Historical Society of Wisconsin (Whi D32 812)

25   Andreas Larsen Dahl, American, b. Norway, 1844–1923, *The Home

of Sjur Reque, Deerfield Township, Dane City, Wisconsin*, 1874, printed later. Gelatin silver print from original glass plate negative, 8 by 10 in. Courtesy State Historical Society of Wisconsin (WhiD31 527)

26   Andreas Larsen Dahl, American, b. Norway, 1844–1923, *Rev. John A. Ottesen house and family, Utica Township, Dane County, Wisconsin*, 1874, printed later. Gelatin silver print from original glass plate negative, 8 by 10 in. Courtesy State Historical Society of Wisconsin (Whi D31 300)

27   Andreas Larsen Dahl, American, b. Norway, 1844–1923, *Portrait of Ever B. Lund and Wife, Blue Mounds, Blue Valley, Wisconsin*, c. 1879, printed later. Gelatin silver print from original glass plate negative, 10 by 8 in. Courtesy State Historical Society of Wisconsin (Whi D32 862)

28   Andreas Larsen Dahl, American, b. Norway, 1844–1923, *Portrait of man and woman, Madison, Wisconsin*, 1879, printed later. Gelatin silver print from original glass plate negative, 10 by 8 in. Courtesy State Historical Society of Wisconsin (Whi D3 92)

29   Andreas Larsen Dahl, American, b. Norway, 1844–1923, *Portrait of a woman with Norwegian trim on collar, Madison, Wisconsin*, c. 1879, printed later. Gelatin silver print from original glass plate negative, 8 by 10 in. Courtesy State Historical Society of Wisconsin (Whi D32 858)

30   Unknown artist, *C. T. Sampson's Shoe Manufactory with Chinese shoemakers in working costume*, c. 1875. Stereograph, 3¹/₁₆ by 6½ in. Courtesy The Stanley B. Burns, M.D. Collection

31   Keller, *"First Blow at the Chinese Question,"* from *The Wasp*, December 8, 1877. Chromogenic print of lithograph, 8 by 10 in. Courtesy Bancroft Library

32   A. J. Russell, American, 1830–1902, *Chinese working on railroad*, 1869, printed later. Gelatin silver print from lantern slide, 8 by 10 in. Courtesy The Oakland Museum History Department

33   J. H. Grady, *"Prayer of the Workingmen of California for Relief!"*, 1880. Printed text, 9⁵/₁₆ by 6¹/₁₆ in. Courtesy Chicago Historical Society

34   Martin Behrman, after Isaiah West Taber, American, 1862–1945, *Miss Cable's class of Chinese girls, Chinatown, San Francisco*, c. 1882, printed later. Gelatin silver print, 6½ by 9½ in. Courtesy California Historical Society, San Francisco (FN-29441)

35   Unknown artist, Untitled (Chinese women on shipboard), c. 1880. Cyanotype, 3¹⁵/₁₆ by 3⁷/₁₆ in. Courtesy The Bancroft Library

36   Solomon D. Butcher, American, 1856–1927, Untitled (the Hilton family, immigrants from England, on their homestead near Weissert, Custer County, Nebraska), c. 1889. Gelatin silver print from glass plate negative, 8 by 10 in. Courtesy Solomon D. Butcher Collection/Nebraska State Historical Society

37   W. F. Song Studio, Untitled (studio portrait of a Chinese woman), San Francisco, c. 1890. Albumen silver print, 8 by 5¹⁵/₁₆ in. Courtesy California Historical Society, San Francisco (FN-19253)

38   Clinch Photography Studio, Untitled (studio portrait of Chinese man), c. 1890. Albumen silver print,

6⅜ by 4⅛ in. Courtesy The Bancroft Library

39   Unknown artist, *Plantation workers*, Hawaii, c. 1890. Albumen silver print, 7⅛ by 9 in. Courtesy Bishop Museum

40   Unknown artist, *Free Trade* (poster proclaiming economic benefits for Irish immigrant mill workers in the New Jersey linen works), c. 1890, printed later. Collotype with text, 21½ by 27¾ in. Courtesy State Historical Society of Wisconsin (5-711)

41   Frederick Burr Opper, American, 1857–1937, *"Castle Garden Emigrant-Catchers,"* from *Puck*, June 14, 1882. Lithograph, 8⁵/₁₆ by 11¾ in. Courtesy Collection of John and Selma Appel, Michigan State University Museum.

42   Jacob A. Riis, American, b. Denmark, 1849–1914, *Home of an Italian ragpicker, Jersey Street*, c. 1894, printed later. Gelatin silver print, 8 by 10 in. Courtesy The Jacob A. Riis Collection, Museum of the City of New York

43   Jacob A. Riis, American, b. Denmark, 1849–1914, *"In Poverty Gap," West 28 Street: an English coal-heaver's home*, c. 1895, printed later. Gelatin silver print, 8 by 10 in. Courtesy The Jacob A. Riis Collection, Museum of the City of New York

44   Jacob A. Riis, American, b. Denmark, 1849–1914, *"Ready for Sabbath Eve in a Coal Cellar," A cobbler in Ludlow Street*, c. 1895, printed later. Gelatin silver print, 8 by 10 in. Courtesy The Jacob A. Riis Collection, Museum of the City of New York

45   Arnold Genthe, American, b. Germany, 1869–1942, *Chinese*

family, c. 1890. Albumen silver print, 13½ by 10⅛ in. Courtesy Private Collection

46   Arnold Genthe, American, b. Germany, 1869–1942, *Street of the Gamblers, Chinatown, San Francisco*, c. 1900. Gelatin silver print, 23 by 17 in. Courtesy California Historical Society, San Francisco (FN-23115)

47   Perry Cutts & Co., *Portrait of Wong Mu Lou*, 1899. Albumen silver print, 5⅜ by 3¹⁵/₁₆ in. Courtesy The Sara Cleary-Burns Collection

48   Unknown artist, *Physical examination, Ellis Island*, c. 1895, printed later. Gelatin silver print, 8 by 10 in. Courtesy National Park Service: Statue of Liberty National Monument

49   Frances B. Johnston, American 1864–1952, Untitled (women and children sitting on deck of *S.S. Amsterdam*), c. 1897. Gelatin silver print, 4 by 5 in. Courtesy Prints and Photographs Division, Library of Congress, Washington DC

50   Grant Hamilton, *"Uncle Sam is a Man of Strong Features,"* from *Judge*, November 26, 1898, vol.35, no.893 (cover illustration). Lithograph, 12 by 10 in. Courtesy Penrose Library, University of Denver

51   Cutbirth Studio, *Portrait of Arig Fou*, 1899. Albumen silver print, 5½ by 3¹⁵/₁₆ in. Courtesy The Sara Cleary-Burns Collection

52   Joseph Judd Pennell, American, 1866–1922, *Tom Allen Cullinan, Junction City, Kansas*, 1901, printed later. Gelatin silver print, 10 by 8 in. Courtesy Joseph J. Pennell Collection, Kansas Collection, University of Kansas Libraries

53   Augustus Sherman, American, 1859?–1925, *Children's Playground, Ellis Island Roof-garden*, c. 1900, printed later. Gelatin silver print, 8 by 10 in. Courtesy The Jacob A. Riis Collection, Museum of the City of New York

54   Augustus Sherman, American, 1859?–1925, *"John D. Third and family, natives of Scotland, S.S. Caledonia, September 17, 1905. Went to friend, John Fleming, Anniston, Alabama,"* printed later. Gelatin silver print, 8 by 10 in. Courtesy National Park Service: Statue of Liberty National Monument

55   Augustus Sherman, American, 1859?–1925, Untitled (Georgian man at Ellis Island), c. 1910. Gelatin silver print, 9½ by 6⅞ in. Courtesy William Williams Papers, Rare Books and Manuscripts Division, New York Public Library, Astor, Lenox and Tilden Foundations

56   Augustus Sherman, American, 1859?–1925, Untitled (two Dutch children at Ellis Island), c. 1910. Gelatin silver print, 9½ by 6½ in. Courtesy William Williams Papers, Rare Books and Manuscripts Division, New York Public Library, Astor, Lenox and Tilden Foundations

57   Augustus Sherman, American, 1959?–1925, *Gypsy family at Ellis Island*, c. 1910. Gelatin silver print, 9½ by 6¾ in. Courtesy William Williams Papers, Rare Books and Manuscripts Division, New York Public Library, Astor, Lenox and Tilden Foundations

58   Augustus Sherman, American, 1859?–1925, Untitled (two Russian children at Ellis Island), c. 1910. Gelatin silver print, 9½ by 7½ in. Courtesy William Williams Papers, Rare Books and Manuscripts Division, New York Public Library, Astor, Lenox and Tilden Foundations

59   Augustus Sherman, American, 1859?–1925, Untitled (Russian man on steps, Ellis Island), c. 1910. Gelatin silver print, 9½ x 6⅞ in. Courtesy William Williams Papers, Rare Books and Manuscripts Division, New York Public Library, Astor, Lenox and Tilden Foundations

60   Augustus Sherman, American, 1859?–1925, Untitled (two Eastern European men at Ellis Island, one playing instrument), c. 1910. Gelatin silver print, 9½ by 6⅞ in. Courtesy William Williams Papers, Rare Books and Manuscripts Division, New York Public Library, Astor, Lenox and Tilden Foundations

61   Augustus Sherman, American, 1859?–1925, *Women from Guadeloupe, French West Indies, at Ellis Island after arrival on* S.S. Korona, 1911. Gelatin silver print, 9½ by 7⅛ in. Courtesy William Williams Papers, Rare Books and Manuscripts Division, New York Public Library, Astor, Lenox and Tilden Foundations

62   Augustus Sherman, American, 1859?–1925, Untitled (three Dutch women at Ellis Island), c. 1910. Gelatin silver print, 9½ by 7⅛ in. Courtesy William Williams Papers, Rare Books and Manuscripts Division, New York Public Library, Astor, Lenox and Tilden Foundations

63   Unknown artist, "*Receiving a letter on board,* S.S. Patricia," 1902, printed later. Gelatin silver print, 8 by 10 in. Courtesy The Byron Collection, Museum of the City of New York

64   Unknown artist, "*Steerage Numbered Ready to Land at Ellis Island,* S.S. Patricia," 1902, printed later. Gelatin silver print, 8 by 10 in. Courtesy The Byron Collection, Museum of the City of New York

65   Unknown artist, "*Dancing in Steerage, S.S. Patricia,*" 1902, printed later. Gelatin silver print, 8 by 10 in. Courtesy The Byron Collection, Museum of the City of New York

66   Unknown artist, *Hungarian immigrant family, Ellis Island,* c. 1900, printed later. Gelatin silver print, 8 by 10 in. Courtesy National Park Service: Statue of Liberty National Monument

67   Boulanger et Frères, Untitled (coal & ice workers, mostly French Canadians, in Manchester, NH), c. 1900, printed later. Gelatin silver print, 5⅞ by 8⅜ in. Courtesy Instructional Services, Dimond Library, University of New Hampshire

68   Unknown artist, *Immigration Battery Park,* 1901, printed later. Gelatin silver print, 8 by 10 in. Courtesy The Byron Collection, Museum of the City of New York

69   Unknown artist, *Americanization class conducted by Board of Education,* c. 1900. Gelatin silver print, 7⁷/₁₆ by 8⁹/₁₆ in. Courtesy Prints and Photographs Division, Library of Congress, Washington DC

70   J. H. Adams, "*Contract Laborers to be Deported," Regulation of Immigration at the Port of Entry, New York City,* 1900. Gelatin silver print, 8⅜ by 7³/₁₆ in. Courtesy Carpenter Center for the Visual Arts, Harvard University

71   J. H. Adams, "*Saved at the Last Moment (Through an Appeal, the Order to Deport was Revoked),*" 1900. Gelatin silver print, 8¼ by 7⅛ in. Courtesy Carpenter Center for the Visual Arts, Harvard University

72   Unknown artist, *Alaska Yukon Pacific Exhibition, Norway Day,* 1909. Gelatin silver print from glass plate negative, 8 by 10 in. Courtesy Museum of History and Industry, Seattle

73   Lewis Hine, American, 1874–1940, *Climbing into America, Ellis Island,* c. 1905/1939–49. Gelatin silver print, 6½ by 4⅞ in. Courtesy Photography Collection, Miriam and Ira D. Wallach Division of Art, Prints and Photographs, The New York Public Library, Astor, Lenox and Tilden Foundations, Gift of Russell Sage

74   Lewis Hine, American, 1874–1940, *Italian Immigrants at Ellis Island,* 1905/1939–49. Gelatin silver print, 6½ by 4⅞ in. Courtesy Photography Collection, Miriam and Ira D. Wallach Division of Art, Prints and Photographs, The New York Public Library, Astor, Lenox and Tilden Foundations, Gift of Russell Sage

75   Lewis Hine, American, 1874–1940, *Albanian Woman, Ellis Island,* 1905. Gelatin silver print, 6³/₁₆ by 4½ in. Courtesy Collection Center for Creative Photography, The University of Arizona

76   Lewis Hine, American, 1874–1940, *Joys and Sorrows at Ellis Island,* 1905/1939–49. Gelatin silver print, 4⅝ by 6½ in. Courtesy Photography Collection, Miriam and Ira D. Wallach Division of Art, Prints and Photographs, The New York Public Library, Astor, Lenox and Tilden Foundations, Gift of Russell Sage

77   Lewis Hine, American, 1874–1940, *Slavic Mother and Child at Ellis Island,* 1905/1939–49. Gelatin silver print, 6⅝ by 4⅝ in. Courtesy Romana Javitz Collection, Photography Collection, Miriam and Ira D. Wallach Division of Art, Prints and Photographs, The New York Public Library, Astor, Lenox and Tilden Foundations

78   Lewis Hine, American, 1874–1940, *Steelworkers at Russian boarding house, Homestead, Pennsylvania*, c. 1907. Gelatin silver print, 4 by 5 in. Courtesy The Joyce and Michael Axelrod Collection

79   Lewis Hine, American, 1874–1940, *Italian Girl at Ellis Island Finds her First Penny*, 1926/1939–49. Gelatin silver print, 4⅞ by 6⅜ in. Courtesy Romana Javitz Collection, Photography Collection, Miriam and Ira D. Wallach Division of Art, Prints and Photographs, The New York Public Library, Astor, Lenox and Tilden Foundations, Gift of Russell Sage

80   Unknown artist, *Finnish lumber crew, Wolf River, Wisconsin*, 1904. Gelatin silver print, 7³/₁₆ by 10⁹/₁₆ in. Courtesy Prints and Photographs Division, Library of Congress, Washington DC

81   Barnes-Crosby Company, *Maxwell Street area*, c. 1905, printed later. Gelatin silver print, 10 by 8 in. Courtesy Chicago Historical Society

82   Unknown artist, *Gouverneur Hospital waiting room, New York City*, 1906, printed later. Gelatin silver print, 10 by 8 in. Courtesy Museum of the City of New York

83   Unknown artist, Untitled (one of the 1000 marriageable girls on the *Baltic*), 1907, printed later. Gelatin silver print, 5 by 7 in. Courtesy Prints and Photographs Division, Library of Congress, Washington DC

84   Unknown artist, *Hester Street, street vendors, New York City*, c. 1909, printed later. Gelatin silver print, 8 by 10 in. Courtesy The Byron Collection, Museum of the City of New York

85   Unknown artist, *Medical examination of arriving aliens by U.S. Public Health Service officers at Ellis Island*, c. 1910. Gelatin silver print, 7¹⁵/₁₆ by 10⅝ in. National Archives, Washington, DC

86   Unknown artist, *African immigrants, Ellis Island*, c. 1910, printed later. Gelatin silver print, 8 by 10 in. Courtesy National Park Service: Statue of Liberty National Monument

87   Unknown artist, *"A General Strike is Declared in the Clothing Industry,"* c. 1910s, printed later. Gelatin silver print, 5 by 7 in. Courtesy Brown Brothers Stock Photos, Sterling, PA

88   Unknown artist, *Chinatown, New York City, New Year, January 30, 1911*, printed later. Gelatin silver print, 8 by 10 in. Courtesy Prints and Photographs Division, Library of Congress, Washington DC

89   F. P. Burke, Untitled (physical examination), from *Infant Welfare Society* series, c. 1910. Gelatin silver print, 9¾ by 14 in. Courtesy Chicago Historical Society

90   Unknown artist, Untitled (women taking children for stroll), from *Infant Welfare Society* series, c. 1910. Gelatin silver print, 10¾ by 13½ in. Courtesy Chicago Historical Society

91   Unknown artist, Untitled (bathing child), from *Infant Welfare Society* series, c. 1915. Gelatin silver print, 10¾ by 13¼ in. Courtesy Chicago Historical Society

92   Unknown artist, Untitled (woman breastfeeding), from *Infant Welfare Society* series, c. 1915. Gelatin silver print, 10½ by 13¾ in. Courtesy Chicago Historical Society

93   Unknown artist, *Interior of Lithuanian bachelor's residence*, c. 1915, printed later. Gelatin silver print, 8 by 10 in. Courtesy Chicago Historical Society

94   Unknown artist, *SE corner of Division & Noble; headquarters of the Kosciusko Guards*, c. 1910s. Gelatin silver print, 9¾ by 7½ in. Courtesy Chicago Historical Society

95   Unknown artist, *Maypole festivity at day nursery at Chicago Commons*, c. 1915. Gelatin silver print, 7 by 9¼ in. Courtesy Chicago Historical Society

96   Unknown artist, *Japanese Boiler Tenders—left to right: Tokutaro Ishimi, Mr. Yamashiro, and Mr. Karasaki, "Hoea" Sugar Mill, Kohala*, c. 1910. Albumen silver print, 3⅞ by 5½ in.   Courtesy Bishop Museum

97   Unknown artist, *Charles Petioni with brother James and sister Blanche from Trinidad and Tobago, British West Indies. Wife Rosa and daughters Muriel and Marguerite joined him a year later*, 1918, printed later. Gelatin silver print, 10 by 8 in. Courtesy Muriel M. Petioni, M.D.

98   Unknown artist, *Cape Verdean immigrants on* S.S. Savoia, *arriving in New Bedford, Massachusetts, October 4, 1914*, printed later. Gelatin silver print, 8 by 10 in. Courtesy Old Dartmouth Historical Society—New Bedford Whaling Museum

99   Kaufmann & Fabry Co., *Americanization class, Adult Education*, 1919. Gelatin silver print, 8 by 10 in. Courtesy Chicago Historical Society

100   Unknown artist, *French war brides on the* Mt. Vernon, *April 4, 1919*. Gelatin silver print, 8 by 10 in. Courtesy Prints and Photographs Division, Library of Congress, Washington DC

101   Kuhli Photo Studio, *Goldie Mabovitz Meyerson—later famous as Golda Meir, Prime Minister of Israel—plays "Liberty" in American Pageant, Milwaukee, Wisconsin, May 18, 1919*. Gelatin silver print, 8 by 10 in. Courtesy State Historical Society of Wisconsin (Whi X3 22831)

102   G. S. Carney, *Czecho-Slovak group, American Pageant, Milwaukee, Wisconsin, May 17–18, 1919*. Gelatin silver print, 8 by 33¼ in. Courtesy State Historical Society of Wisconsin (Whi X31 17483)

103   Unknown artist, *Aliens arriving, Angel Island Quarantine Station, California, September, 1931*. Gelatin silver print, 8⁹/₁₆ by 10⁹/₁₆ in. Courtesy National Archives, Washington, DC

104   L. E. Edgeworth, American, active 1910s–1920s, *Chung Puu and Hawaiian Wife and Family*, 1920. Gelatin silver print, 7⅜ by 9 in. Courtesy Bishop Museum

105   Unknown artist, *U.S. Public Health Officers making quarantine inspection of passengers on a trans-Pacific liner from the Orient, Angel Island, February, 1924*. Gelatin silver print, 8¹/₁₆ by 10⅝ in. Courtesy National Archives, Washington, DC

106   Unknown artist, *Norwegian celebration at Humboldt Park, Chicago*, 1929. Gelatin silver print, 11½ by 9¾ in. Courtesy Chicago Historical Society

107   Hugo L. Summerville, American, 1885–1948, *The C. Campa Labor Agency and W. J. Lewis of the Alamo City Employment Agency, distributing bread three times a day to Mexicans who are in distress waiting to be sent to a job, March 22, 1924*, printed later. Gelatin silver print, 9¾ by 33½ in. Courtesy Photography Collection, Harry Ransom Humanities Research Center, The University of Texas at Austin

108   Eugene Omar Goldbeck, American, 1892–1986, *Immigration Border Patrol, Laredo, Texas, February, 1926, M. M. Hanson, Inspector in charge*, printed later. Gelatin silver print, 9¾ by 40⅜ in. Courtesy Photography Collection, Harry Ransom Humanities Research Center, The University of Texas at Austin

109   Eugene Omar Goldbeck, American, 1892–1986, *Einstein at the Grand Canyon*, 1922. Gelatin silver print, 7¼ by 8¹⁵/₁₆ in. Collection Museum of Photographic Arts, Gift of Terry Etherton

110   Unknown artist, Untitled (Japanese-American congregation, Utah), 1931. Gelatin silver print, 7½ by 9½ in. Courtesy Amistad Research Center, Tulane University, New Orleans, LA

111   Unknown artist, Untitled (Japanese-American baseball team, Seattle), 1931. Gelatin silver print, 3¼ by 5½ in. Courtesy Amistad Research Center, Tulane University, New Orleans, LA

112   Arthur Rothstein, American, 1915–1985, *Mexican rehabilitation clients, Dona Ana County, New Mexico*, 1936, printed later. Gelatin silver print, 8 by 10 in. Courtesy Prints and Photographs Division, Library of Congress, Washington DC

113   Unknown artist, Untitled (Fannie Lui, Effie Lui, and Elizabeth Ng, Grace Faith Church, New York City), c. 1937. Gelatin silver print, 6¾ by 4¾ in. Courtesy Chinatown History Museum, Gift of Fannie Lui

114   Dorothea Lange, American, 1895–1965, *Braceros*, c. 1938. Gelatin silver print, 10¼ by 9½ in. Courtesy The Oakland Museum, Gift of Paul S. Taylor

115   Russell Lee, American, 1903–1986, *Daughter of a Mexican farm family at home. Portraits of the family are above her, Santa Maria, Texas*, 1939, printed later. Gelatin silver print, 10 by 8 in. Courtesy Prints and Photographs Division, Library of Congress, Washington DC

116   Alexander Alland, American, b. Russia, 1902–1989, *Home of Gypsies on Hester Street*, 1940. Gelatin silver print, 11 by 10 in. Courtesy Howard Greenberg Gallery, New York

117   Russell Lee, American, 1903–1986, *Mexican-American group at fiesta, Taos, New Mexico*, 1940, printed later. Gelatin silver print, 8 by 10 in. Courtesy Prints and Photographs Division, Library of Congress, Washington DC

118   Unknown artist, *FBI going through the belongings of a Japanese American family*, 1942, printed later. Gelatin silver print, 8 by 10 in. Courtesy Department of Special Collections, University Research Library, University of California, Los Angeles (#27.459)

119   Clem Albers, *A young evacuee of Japanese ancestry waits with the family baggage before leaving by bus for an assembly center, Los Angeles, April, 1942*. Gelatin silver print, 5 by 7 in. Courtesy National Archives, Washington, DC

120   Ansel Adams, American, 1902–1984, *Still life, Yonemitsu family quarters, Manzanar Relocation Center, California, October 1943*, from *Born Free and Equal*. Gelatin silver print, 8⅞ by 5⁹/₁₆ in. Courtesy Collection Center for Creative Photography, The University of Arizona

121   Unknown artist, Untitled (U.S. Government propaganda photo of woman sewing American flag in Manzanar), c. 1943. Gelatin silver print, 11 by 14 in. Courtesy The Oakland Museum History Department

122   John Vachon, American, 1914–1975, *Mexican and Negro farm labor, Corpus Christi, Texas*, 1943, printed later. Gelatin silver print, 8 by 10 in. Courtesy Prints and Photographs Division, Library of Congress, Washington DC

123   Gordon Parks, American, b. 1912, *Forging crew at the Fafnir Bearing Company, New Britain, Connecticut. Left to right: John Evanowski, Polish; Charles Kochan, Polish; Walter Velicka, Lithuanian; and Albert Zils, German-American*, 1943, printed later. Gelatin silver print, 8 by 10 in. Courtesy Prints and Photographs Division, Library of Congress, Washington DC

124   Unknown artist, *"Swedish Love of Land, Freedom Thrives in U.S.,"* from *Victory*, v.1, n.2, May 13, 1943. Printed text with black & white photographs, 21 by 14 in. Courtesy National Archives, Washington, DC

125   Unknown artist, *"German Blood—but in American Hearts,"* from *Victory*, v.1, n.1, April 21, 1943, pp. 30–31. Printed text with black & white photographs, 21 by 14 in. Courtesy National Archives, Washington, DC

126   Hikiru Iwasaki, *Japanese workers, relocated during WWII, working at Chicago Vegetable Packing House*, 1944. Gelatin silver print, 8 by 10 in. Courtesy Chicago Historical Society

127   Unknown artist, *Panorama of Japanese American women soldiers, Fort Snelling*, 1945. Gelatin silver print, 8 by

22½ in. Courtesy Toyome Nakanishi Collection, National Japanese American Historical Society, San Francisco

128   Burt Glinn, American, b. 1925, *Swearing-in of new citizens on Battleship* Missouri, *Seattle, Washington*, 1954, printed later. Gelatin silver print, 11 by 14 in. Courtesy the artist

129   Burt Glinn, American, b. 1925, *Alien registration, New York City*, c. 1950s, printed later. Gelatin silver print, 11 by 14 in. Courtesy the artist

130   Unknown artist, *Cuban refugees*, c. 1964, printed later. Gelatin silver print, 11 by 14 in. Courtesy Historical Association of Southern Florida

131   Charles Trainor, *Airlift list of Cuban refugees*, 1970, printed later. Gelatin silver print, 11 by 14 in. Courtesy Historical Association of Southern Florida, Miami News Collection

132   Pok Chi Lau, American, b. Hong Kong, 1950, *Toi-Sahn Chinese girl watching cartoons at home, San Francisco*, from *Asian Migration* series, 1976. Gelatin silver print, 16 by 20 in. Courtesy the artist

133   Pok Chi Lau, American, b. Hong Kong, 1950, *Nude beauty pictures in the bedroom of a Vietnamese Chinese newly wedded couple. The grandfather is eating in the kitchen, San Francisco*, from *Asian Migration* series, 1981. Gelatin silver print, 16 by 20 in. Courtesy the artist

134   Pok Chi Lau, American, b. Hong Kong, 1950, *Tyler Kakeru Lau, son of the photographer, first day as an Asian American, Lawrence, Kansas*, from *Asian Migration* series, 1988. Gelatin silver print, 16 by 20 in. Courtesy the artist

135   Unknown artist, *Cuban refugees with varied expressions look at American*

coast, off Key West. Coast Guard cutter Diligence *in background*, c. 1980. Gelatin silver print, 11 by 14 in. Courtesy Historical Association of Southern Florida

136   Unknown artist, *Haitian refugees*, c. 1980. Gelatin silver print, 11 by 14 in. Courtesy Historical Association of Southern Florida

137   Mel Rosenthal, American, b. 1948, *Cambodian refugee children in the South Bronx, August 1983*, from *Refugee* series. Gelatin silver print, 20 by 16 in. Courtesy the artist

138   Mel Rosenthal, American, b. 1948, *Two Cambodian businessmen with a Buddhist monk at a celebration at the Church Avenue Refugee Center, Brooklyn, New York, April 1985*, from *Refugee* series. Gelatin silver print, 16 by 20 in. Courtesy the artist

139   Mel Rosenthal, American, b. 1948, *A Buddhist monastery, Marion Avenue, the Bronx, September 1985*, from *Refugee* series. Gelatin silver print, 16 by 20 in. Courtesy the artist

140   Mel Rosenthal, American, b. 1948, *Two women of the Hmong community, Syracuse, New York, May 1992*, from *Refugee* series. Gelatin silver print, 20 by 16 in. Courtesy the artist

141   Mark J. Sindler, American, b. 1954, *Home altar, Versailles Community, New Orleans, Louisiana, 1979*, from *The Vietnamese Documentary Project*. Gelatin silver print, 11½ by 8 in. Courtesy the artist

142   Ulli Steltzer, German, b. 1923, *Volunteers of the Holt Adoption Agency carry Korean babies off a plane at Los Angeles International Airport*, 1983. Gelatin silver print, 20 by 16 in. Courtesy the artist

143 Ulli Steltzer, German, b. 1923, *Cambodian dance class in a Long Beach beauty shop*, from *The New Americans*, 1984. Gelatin silver print, 20 by 16 in. Courtesy the artist

144 Audrey Gottlieb, American, b. 1944, *Brahmin priest chants and lays clay Ganesha elephant god into muddy bed of Flushing Meadow Lake, Queens, New York*, from *Cosmopolitan Queens* series, c. 1990. Chromogenic print, 16 by 20 in. Courtesy the artist

145 Audrey Gottlieb, American, b. 1944, *Geeta Hindu Temple celebration*, from *Cosmopolitan Queens* series, c. 1990. Chromogenic print, 16 by 20 in. Courtesy the artist

146 Audrey Gottlieb, American, b. 1944, *Indian housewife paints 'rangoli' design at front entrance to her house, Queens, New York*, from *Cosmopolitan Queens* series, c. 1990. Chromogenic print, 16 by 20 in. Courtesy the artist

147 Audrey Gottlieb, American, b. 1944, *Wrapping the Sikh turban, Gurdwara Temple, Richmond Hill, Queens, New York*, from *Cosmopolitan Queens* series, c. 1990. Chromogenic print, 16 by 20 in. Courtesy the artist

148 Audrey Gottlieb, American, b. 1944, *Bagpipers bleat Irish Americans to prayer at St. Sebastian's Church, Woodside, Queens, New York*, from *Cosmopolitan Queens* series c. 1990. Chromogenic print, 16 by 20 in. Courtesy the artist

149 Rick Rocamora, American, b. Philippines, 1947, *Sergio Quinial, 68, with a picture of himself at age 21, hand-carried when he left the Philippines. "We can solve all our problems here in America except loneliness,"* 1993. Gelatin silver print, 14 by 11 in. Courtesy the artist

150 Rick Rocamora, American, b. Philippines, 1947, *"God Bless America" (Filipino World War II veterans wave the American flag while singing "God Bless America" during naturalization ceremonies in San Francisco Marriot Hotel)*, 1993. Gelatin silver print, 14 by 11 in. Courtesy the artist

151 Donna DeCesare, American, b. 1955, *Grand Rapids, Michigan*, 1992. Gelatin silver print, 14 by 17 in. Courtesy the artist

152 Donna DeCesare, American, b. 1955, *Los Angeles Pico Union*, 1993. Gelatin silver print, 14 by 17 in. Courtesy the artist

153 Maggie Steber, American, b. 1949, *Wedding reception at the Big Five Country Club (which upper class Cubans belong to in an effort to hold onto their culture, Florida)*, 1991. Chromogenic print, 16 by 20 in. Courtesy the artist

154 Alex Webb, American, b. 1952, *Christmas pageant, Cuban Social Club, Miami*, 1988. Cibachrome print, 16 by 20 in. Courtesy the artist

155 Alex Webb, American, b. 1952, *Cubans training, Everglades*, 1988. Cibachrome print, 16 by 20 in. Courtesy the artist

156 Alex Webb, American, b. 1952, *Central American refugees, near Brownsville, Texas*, c. 1989. Cibachrome print, 16 by 20 in. Courtesy the artist

157 Alex Webb, American, b. 1952, *I.N.S. Krome Detention Center, Miami, Florida*, 1988. Cibachrome print, 16 by 20 in. Courtesy the artist

158 Alex Webb, American, b. 1952, *Arrest, San Ysidro, California*, 1979. Cibachrome print, 16 by 20 in. Courtesy the artist

159 Alex Webb, American, b. 1952, *Guatemalan immigrants, Indiantown*, 1988. Cibachrome print, 16 by 20 in. Courtesy the artist

160 Gary Monroe, American, b. 1951, *I.N.S. Krome Detention Camp, Miami*, 1981. Gelatin silver print, 16 by 20 in. Courtesy the artist

161 Gary Monroe, American, b. 1951, *Men's Building #8, I.N.S. Krome Detention Center, Miami*, 1981. Gelatin silver print, 16 by 20 in. Courtesy the artist

162 Gary Monroe, American, b. 1951, *Fort Pierce, Florida*, 1994. Gelatin silver print, 16 by 20 in. Courtesy the artist,

163 Leonard Freed, American, b. 1929, Untitled, Wausau, Wisconsin, 1994. Gelatin silver print, 11 by 14 in. Courtesy the artist, Magnum Photos

164 Pablo Delano, American, b. Puerto Rico, 1954, *Maternity counselor, ASPIRA, South Bronx*, 1986. Gelatin silver print, 14 by 11 in. Courtesy the artist

165 Pablo Delano, American, b. Puerto Rico, 1954, *Outside Sabater Grocery at dusk, El Barrio, New York City*, 1988. Gelatin silver print, 16 by 20 in. Courtesy the artist

166 Dave Gatley, American, b. 1943, *Three ghostly figures emerge from behind a hill, as seen on the screen of an infra-red scope used to penetrate the almost total darkness near the border. Their movements will be radioed to the nearest Border Patrol unit*, 1992. Chromogenic print, 8 by 10 in. Courtesy the artist, *Los Angeles Times*

167 Dave Gatley, American, b. 1943, *This illegal alien crawls through*

the gate mechanism to check on La Migra *(The Border Patrol), before he helps funnel others across the gated area,* 1992. Chromogenic print, 11 by 14 in. Courtesy the artist, *Los Angeles Times*

168   Don Bartletti, American, b. 1947, *Pedestrian Barrier and Warning Sign,* 1993. Chromogenic print, 16 by 20 in. Courtesy the artist, *Los Angeles Times*

169   Don Bartletti, American, b. 1947, *Interstate Pedestrians,* 1989. Digital print, 16 by 20 in. Courtesy the artist, *Los Angeles Times*

170   Don Bartletti, American, b. 1947, *Survival Class,* 1988. Digital print, 16 by 20 in. Courtesy the artist, *Los Angeles Times*

171   Don Bartletti, American, b. 1947, *Border Opinions,* 1991. Digital print, 16 by 20 in. Courtesy the artist, *Los Angeles Times*

172   Don Bartletti, American, b. 1947, *Highway Camp, Encinitas, California,* 1989. Gelatin silver print, 16 by 20 in. Collection Museum of Photographic Arts, Gift of the artist

173   Don Bartletti, American, b. 1947, *Lupe Villasenor and Son Victor,* 1991. Chromogenic print, 8 by 10 in. Courtesy the artist

174   Kira Corser, American, b. 1951, *Children at candlelight vigil protesting closure of Migrant Farmworker Camp, Carlsbad, California,* 1989. Gelatin silver print, 14 by 10½ in. Courtesy the artist

175   Richard Steven Street, American, b. 1946, *Canyon dwellers waiting for work beneath steel signs erected by city residents discouraging people*

from hiring them, Alpine, California, from *Organizing for Our Lives,* 1992. Gelatin silver print, 14 by 11 in. Courtesy the artist

176   Richard Steven Street, American, b. 1946, *Men pulling strawberry plants through holes burned in plastic cover, Gilroy, California,* from *Organizing for Our Lives,* 1992. Gelatin silver print, 11 by 14 in. Courtesy the artist

177   Ira Nowinski, American, b. 1942, *Toba Weiss, immigrant from Russia, with photographs of her brother taken on his arrival in Auschwitz, taken in San Francisco,* c. 1984. Gelatin silver print, 20 by 16 in. Courtesy the artist

178   Ira Nowinski, American, b. 1942, *Celebration of 9th of May (victory of Socialism over Fascism), Jewish Community Center, San Francisco,* from *Russian Jews: A Documentary,* c. 1984. Gelatin silver print, 20 by 16 in. Courtesy the artist

179   Chester Higgins, Jr., American, b. 1946, *Memorial to African ancestors who perished in Atlantic Ocean during transfer from Africa to American enslavement,* 1990. Gelatin silver print, 16 by 20 in. Courtesy the artist

180   Chester Higgins, Jr., American, b. 1946, *Asante King from Ghana, Diaspora King seated in court,* 1988. Gelatin silver print, 16 by 20 in. Courtesy the artist

181   Chester Higgins, Jr., American, b. 1946, *Brazilian immigrant worships Oshun, African deity of fresh water and love,* 1989. Gelatin silver print, 16 by 20 in. Courtesy the artist

182   Sebastião Salgado, Brazilian, b. 1944, *Russians waiting in Moscow airport,* 1994. Gelatin silver print, 16 by 20 in. Courtesy the artist

183   Sebastião Salgado, Brazilian, b. 1944, *Russian sauna in Brooklyn,* 1994. Gelatin silver print, 16 by 20 in. Courtesy the artist

184   James Newberry, American, b. 1937, *A & H Factory for Alternators-Starters-Batteries—Mr. Ahmed Elhadary, born in Cairo, Egypt,* from *Changing Chicago* series, 1987. Chromogenic print, 9½ by 9½ in. Courtesy Chicago Historical Society

185   James Newberry, American, b. 1937, *Grandfather and children at Japanese street festival. The children's father is of Japanese ancestry. Their mother is of European ancestry,* from *Changing Chicago* series, 1987. Chromogenic print, 9½ by 9½ in. Courtesy Chicago Historical Society

186   James Newberry, American, b. 1937, *Mr. Mohamad Ali, b. Jerusalem presently residing in Detroit, visits Al-Rashid Bakery, 3255 W. 63rd Street, Chicago,* from *Changing Chicago* series, 1987. Chromogenic print, 9½ by 9½ in. Courtesy Chicago Historical Society

187   James Newberry, American, b. 1937, *Monks of Thai Buddhist Temple,* from the *Changing Chicago* series, 1987. Chromogenic print, 6¼ by 6¼ in. Courtesy Chicago Historical Society

188   James Newberry, American, b. 1937, *Ten Ren Tea and Ginseng Company of Chicago Ltd, 2247 S. Wentworth Avenue with Shumen Fine, Owner's wife, born in Taiwan,* from the *Changing Chicago* series, 1987. Chromogenic print, 9½ by 9½ in. Courtesy Chicago Historical Society

189   James Newberry, American, b. 1937, *Slaughter of goats on the feast of Abraham. Mr. Mohammad Mazhar Hussaini (l.), Executive Dir. of the Islamic*

Food and Nutrition Council of America and Director of Halal Slaughter Certification Committee, supervising the Halal slaughter, from the *Changing Chicago* series, 1987. Chromogenic print, 9½ by 9½ in. Courtesy Chicago Historical Society

190   James Newberry, American, b. 1937, *Officers of the student body of the American Islamic College in the mosque of the college. The four are from Syria, Libya, Kuwait, and Jordan (Palestinian),* from the *Changing Chicago* series, 1987. Chromogenic print, 9½ by 9½ in. Courtesy Chicago Historical Society

191   James Newberry, American, b. 1937, *Msgr. John Naffah, pastor and founder of Our Lady of Lebanon Maronite Catholic Church of Chicago, 425 N. Hillside Ave. Hillside, IL., born in Jounieh, Lebanon,* from the *Changing Chicago* series, 1987. Chromogenic print, 9½ by 9½ in. Courtesy Chicago Historical Society

192   James Newberry, American, b. 1937, *Indian father and two sons at Hari Krishna Temple. It is after midnight, following the celebration of Krishna's birthday,* from the *Changing Chicago* series, 1987. Chromogenic print, 9½ by 9½ in. Courtesy Chicago Historical Society

193   James Newberry, American, b. 1937, *Cambodian bride and groom at the conclusion of their day-and-a-half long wedding ceremony, which took place in a small apartment,* from the *Changing Chicago* series, 1987. Chromogenic print, 6½ by 6½ in. Courtesy Chicago Historical Society

194   James Newberry, American, b. 1937, *Fujima Shunojo, Japanese classical dance instructor, and troupe after a performance at a Japanese street festival,* from the *Changing Chicago* series, 1987. Chromogenic print, 9½ by 9½ in. Courtesy Chicago Historical Society

195   Yale Strom, American, b. 1957, *Young girl from Bangladesh, Lower East Side, New York City,* 1995. Gelatin silver print, 11 by 14 in. Courtesy the artist

196   Yale Strom, American, b. 1957, *Young girl from Palestine (West Bank), Dearborn, Michigan,* 1995. Gelatin silver print, 11 by 14 in. Courtesy the artist

197   Yale Strom, American, b. 1957, *Three young girls from Dominican Republic, Lower East Side, New York City,* 1995. Gelatin silver print, 11 by 14 in. Courtesy the artist

198   Yale Strom, American, b. 1957, *Young girl from Yemen, Dearborn, Michigan,* 1995. Gelatin silver print, 11 by 14 in. Courtesy the artist

199   David McNew, American, b. 1953, *Chinese boat people endure the long wait at sea, now watched over by masked US Coast Guard personnel,* 1993. Chromogenic print, 11 by 14 in. Courtesy the artist

200   David McNew, American, b. 1953, *U.S. Coast Guard man throws a blanket to Chinese boat people,* 1993. Chromogenic print, 11 by 14 in. Courtesy the artist

201   Eric Chu, American, b. 1969, *Paradise (vacationers from Westchester County, New York, sit next to their inner tubes while watching as a Cuban raft is cleared off the beach in affluent Boca Raton, Florida, August 24, 1994).* Chromogenic print, 8 by 10 in. Courtesy the artist, *The News* (Boca Raton, FL)

202   Walter Michot, American, b. 1951, *Cuban rafters in open sea,* 1994. Chromogenic print, 11 by 14 in. Courtesy the artist, *The Miami Herald*

203   Walter Michot, American, b. 1951, *Finally ashore (Cuban raft on Florida beach),* 1994. Chromogenic print, 11 by 14 in. Courtesy the artist, *The Miami Herald*

204   Unknown Artist, *Club Prima,* International Correspondence Services, vol.III, ed.II, 1995. Printed text with photographs, 10¾ by 8¼ in. Courtesy Private Collection

ACKNOWLEDGEMENTS

POINTS OF ENTRY has been an extraordinary project, four years in the making, a collaboration of three museums in different cities. This project is comprised of eighty-eight artists, 407 photographic works of art, 330 loan agreements from around the country. Behind the statistics, the artistic and administrative management of the project has encompassed virtually all staff members of the consortium institutions: from curatorial to exhibit design, public relations and fundraising, to education programming, financial and project management, this effort was conceived, developed, coordinated, and produced by thirty people.

POINTS OF ENTRY was created with the guidance and support of the Lila Wallace-Reader's Digest Fund. I wish to acknowledge them for their vision, generosity, and inspiration. Sibyl Jacobson, President and C.E.O., and Irene Wong, Program Associate of Metropolitan Life Foundation, stepped forward to provide additional funding for the national tour and its promotion at a time when substantial corporate recognition was most needed.

My colleagues, Terence Pitts, Director of the Center for Creative Photography in Tucson, Arizona, and Andy Grundberg, Director of The Friends of Photography/Ansel Adams Center for Photography in San Francisco, California, deserve my thanks and gratitude for agreeing to dive into these uncharted waters and commit their energies, talents, and resources to this groundbreaking project: a three-institution, three-city, three-exhibition, three-catalogue production with national, regional, and local programming. Their respective staff members are to be commended for their hard work and dedication toward creating their respective parts of POINTS OF ENTRY.

My co-curator and essayist Vicki Goldberg has made the project come to life by researching eastern archives and uncovering much of the most important art in *A Nation of Strangers.* I had always hoped to find a way for us to collaborate, and I would work with her again in an instant.

A project of this magnitude, on a subject so intrinsic to the United States, could not be developed without offering museum visitors an opportunity to study the subject of immigration beyond the issues presented in POINTS OF

ENTRY itself. The bibliography was researched and compiled by a most knowledgeable individual, Catherine S. Herlihy, Catalogue & Systems Librarian at California State University/San Marcos. I am deeply grateful for her tremendous contribution to this catalogue.

All of the Museum of Photographic Arts' staff were involved with POINTS OF ENTRY for several strenuous years. My particular thanks go to Administrative Director Cathy Silvern Boemer for her tireless shepherding of the myriad details and timelines, and endless diplomacy along the trail; Registrar Henrietta Tye, who developed a thick file around every piece of artwork in the show, and at least as many again that were eventually not included — there are not sufficient words of gratitude for her efforts; Development Director M. Diane Ballard who, along with her predecessor, Richard Perry, raised the substantial funding to attempt a work of this scale; and Curator Diana Gaston, who over and over again helped to clarify ideas as they erupted, and created the extensive and nourishing educational programs that will help to insert this work into the community's dialogue.

During the course of four years of research for this project, innumerable individuals from around the country provided guidance, advice, and recommendations, referrals and encouragement, and, in many cases, loans of original artwork. They include Dina Abramowicz, YIVO Institute for Jewish Research; John and Selma Appel, Terry Ariano, Museum of the City of New York; Diana Areccho, New York Historical Society; Joyce and Michael Axelrod; Don Bartletti; Charles Biasny-Rivera; Ronald P. Bird; Mary Jean Blasdale, New Bedford Whaling Museum; Lynn Bodnar, New York Historical Society; Mary Bowling, New York Public Library; Nicolette Bromberg, State Historical Society of Wisconsin; Louise Brownell, Chicago Historical Society; Charlotte Brown, UCLA Library, Special Collections; Stanley B. Burns, M.D. and Sara Cleary-Burns; John Carter, Nebraska State Historical Society; Carrie Chalmers, Magnum Photos; Ray Collins, Brown Brothers Stock Photos; Adrienne Cooper, Chinatown History Museum; Eric Chu; Kira Corser; Diana Pardue Crane, National Park Service;

Verna Curtis, Library of Congress; Donna DeCesare; Pablo Delano; Jeffery S. Dosik, National Park Service; Timothy Eaton, Boca Raton Museum of Art; Gary Edwards; Phyllis Epstein; Marcia Eymann, The Oakland Museum; David Finn; Roy Flukinger, Harry Ransom Humanities Research Center; Leonard Freed; Merry Foresta; Mary Ann Forssblad, Museum of History and Industry, Seattle; Tomas Ybarra Frausto, Rockefeller Foundation; Jonathan Friedlander; Tom Frye, Penrose Library; Selwyn Garraway; Dave Gatley; Caryn Gedell, New York Public Library; Burt Glinn; Manuel Gonzalez; Audrey Gottlieb; Louis Grachos; Ursula Gropper; Ramón Gutiérrez; Abigail Heyman; Chester Higgins, Jr.; Elizabeth L. Hill, National Archives; Maryl Hosking, New York Public Library; Dawn Hugh, Historical Museum of Southern Florida; Anita Jacobson, Lower East Side Tenement Museum; Drew Johnson, The Oakland Museum; Tambra Johnson, Library of Congress; Betty Lou Kam, Bishop Museum Archives; Andy Kraushaar, State Historical Society of Wisconsin; Michael Kurtz, National Archives and Records; Maxime Lafantasie, Fales Library, New York University; Kathy Lafferty, University of Kansas Libraries, Kansas Collection; Marguerite Lavin, Museum of the City of New York; John H. Lawrence, Historic New Orleans Collection; Gavin Lee; Janet Lehr; Mei-lin Liu, Chinatown History Museum; Sally Livingston, Library of Congress; Karen Lovass, Minnesota Historical Society; Robert MacKimmie, California Historical Society; Janice Madhue, George Eastman House; Mary Ellen Mark; David McNew; Alix Mellis, Howard Greenberg Gallery; Walter Michot; Gary Monroe; Barry Moreno, Ellis Island Library; Nick Natanson, National Archives; Marie Nelson, MoPA volunteer extraordinaire; Dianne Nilson, Center for Creative Photography; Leslie Nolan, Museum of the City of New York; Barbara Norfleet, Carpenter Center for the Visual Arts; Ira Nowinski; Richard Ogar, Bancroft Library; Octavio Olvera, UCLA Library, Special Collections; Ann Patera, Harry Ransom Humanities Research Center; Kara Paw-Pa, National Japanese American Historical Society; Bennett Peji; Muriel H. Petioni, M.D.; François Piffard; Tony Pisani, Museum of the City of New York; Leroy V. Quintana; Bernard Riley; Fred Ritchin; Rick Rocamora; Walter and Naomi Rosenblum; Jeff L. Rosenheim, Metropolitan Museum of Art; Mel Rosenthal; Jeff Rosenwald; Sebastião Salgado; Gary

Samson, Dimond Library, University of New Hampshire; Geraldine Santoro, New York Public Library; Mark J. Sindler; Ellen Smart; Ellen Smith, American Jewish Historical Society; Diane Spielmann, Leo Baeck Institute; Carrie Springer, Howard Greenberg Gallery; Brenda Square, Amistad Research Center, Tulane University; Maggie Steber; Ulli Stelzer; Richard Steven Street; Yale Strom; Manny Strumpf, Public Affairs Officer for the City of New York; Anne Sullivan, Center for Creative Photography; Lynne Swanson, Michigan State University Museum; Ronald Takaki; Marvin Taylor, Fales Library, New York University; Roslyn Tonai, National Japanese American Historical Society; Julia Van Haaften, New York Public Library; Larry Viskochil, Chicago Historical Society; Alex Webb; J. F. Webb; Marek Web, YIVO Institute for Jewish Research; Deborah Willis, Director, African American Museum Project at the Smithsonian Institute; Bonnie Wilson, Minnesota Historical Society; and James Zeender, National Archives and Records.

I thank the Board of Trustees at the Museum of Photographic Arts for providing the ongoing stability and confidence in my staff and me to allow us to attempt daunting tasks and take risks, for the chance to make a real contribution.

At the Museum of Photographic Arts, team-work is a particular strength of my staff, in addition to exceptional grace under pressure, dedication, and the ability to give heart and soul without hesitation when it is needed most. Beyond the work implied by their respective titles, the staff's creativity, professionalism, enthusiasm, and faith in both me, personally, and in POINTS OF ENTRY as an important contribution to our community, are profoundly important to me. Of particular note, I wish to thank M. Diane Ballard, Development Director; Gayle Benn, Public Relations Director; Cathy Silvern Boemer, Administrative Director; Louis Frye, Exhibition Designer; Diana Gaston, Curator; David Kinney, Museum Store Manager; Tomoko Maruyama, NEA Intern; Ilene Mittman, Business Manager; Monica Schaffer, Intern; and Henrietta Tye, Registrar. In addition, Julius Edoh, Buffy Fuller, Phil and Margaret Ham, Ann Laddon, Marisol Lopez, An Nguyen, Kate Palese, Angela Rockett, Helene Samische, and Penny Taylor all helped by keeping the ship steady.

Former staff members who participated in the original planning and early stages of creating POINTS OF ENTRY included Julia Blinn, Dave Eliot, Michael Golino, Jessica O'Dwyer, and Richard Perry, who worked with me to write the original project proposal.

The significant education and community programming created for this project takes place on a local, regional, and national level. Educators' packets, teacher workshops, lectures, speakers' series, film series, artist/community dialogues, docent tours, and school tours are all planned, coordinated, and implemented by the consortium institution's team of curatorial and education professionals. Special thanks to Stevie Mack for coordinating and editing the educators' packets, and to the education advisory committee who guided the MoPA staff in developing the educators' packets and recommending local programming: Linda Burritt, Dr. Gail Guth, Susan Holtz, Virginia Maggio, Carrie McIver, Larry Oviatt, Penny Patten, Al Rodriguez, Louise Russell, Rasheed Salahuddin, Kay Wagner, and Mark Wolfe.

Public relations, advertising, and marketing support for the project has been generously provided by MoPA Trustee, James S. Matthews, and the creative staff of Capener, Matthews and Walcher. Special assistance was provided by another MoPA Trustee, Arnold J. Kleiner, General Manager, KFMB Broadcast Stations in the development of public service announcements.

My interest in pursuing the abundant loose threads of immigration history into a dense and complex web was kindled by thoughts of my grandparents and relatives of my wife, who were themselves immigrants from Europe. Endless conversations with my parents, Benn and Shirley Ollman, about the vicissitudes of the great crossing and the tenuousness of adaptation, set the table for this feast. I thank my wife, Leah, for her enormous encouragement and perfect proofing. I thank my children, Ariel and Jonah, for the time with me that they gave up, unaware that they were assisting me in the creation of a project and text that will help them, as they grow, to understand this place and how they and their neighbors came to be here.

Arthur Ollman, Director
Museum of Photographic Arts